SOCIAL MOVEMENTS IN NORTHEAST INDIA

SOCIAL MOVEMENTS IN NORTHEAST INDIA

Edited By

Sarthak Sengupta

GYAN

Published, 2019

Published by

Gyan Publishing House
5, Ansari Road
Daryaganj, New Delhi-110002
Phone: 011-47034999, 9811692060
www.gyanbooks.com
E-mail: books@gyanbooks.com

Printed at: G. Print Process, Delhi.

Cataloging in Publication Data—DK
Courtesy: D.K. Agencies (P) Ltd. <docinfo@dkagencies.com>

Social movements in Northeast India / edited by Dr. Sarthak Sengupta.
pages cm
Contributed articles.
Includes bibliographical references.
ISBN 9788121214490

1. Social movements—India, Northeastern. I. Sengupta, Sarthak, 1955- editor.

LCC HN690.N67S63 2018 | DDC 303.48409541 23

Dedicated
to the cherished memory of
my elder sister
Late Sukla Roy

CONTENTS

PREFACE

The term 'social movement'was first introduced by a German economist Lorenz von Stein in 1848. It is a characteristic feature of transition, a conscious attempt of masses of people to bring about modification in the social structure by collective action.There is an intimate relationship between social movement and social change. The social movements may be individual or societal; reformative or radical type; subjective or objective; innovative or conservative; violent or non-violent, local or global. Social movements may be categorized into four types – alternative, redemptive, reformative, and revolutionary. The first two are at the individual level, and advocate for minor (alternative) and radial changes (redemptive) respectively; whereas reformative and revolutionary occur at thesocietal level and advocate for minor (reformative) and radical (revolutionary) changes. The social movement generate social unrest as well as social mobility. Hence it has both negative and positive consequence in the society.

The Northeast region of India is one of the most sensitive area of the country for its strategic locations. Most of the social movements in the context of Northeast India have politico-historical dimensions. Although the region witnessesseveral social movements over the centuries, however, it is only recently that social scientists have begun to study its textual and contextual significance in depth. Intensive case studies need to be carried out on different types of social movements to make the people more educated about the multifarious dimensions of different manner to link these ideas with the civil society.

The inspiring collection of research articles accommodated in the present treatise includes twelve contributions by eminent social scientists on varied dimensions of social movements prevailing in Northeast India.The effort expended in compiling this volume will be well rewarded if these articles can provide a glimpse of the social movements in the context of NortheastIndia and prove to be informative and arouse interest to scholars and academicians whoare concerned to study Northeast India in general and those who pursue social movements and civil society as well as political affairs in particular.

19th October 2018 **Sarthak Sengupta**

Acknowledgements

I am deeply beholden to all the distinguished contributors for their unalloyed cooperation and honest support towards this anthology and everyone who had encouraged and assisted me in compiling this volume. Without their kind scholastic cooperation, this academic course of action would never be possible. I extend my heartfelt indebtedness to all of them.

I avail of this opportunity to express my thanks to the authorities of Dibrugarh University for providing the infrastructure facilities. An editor's family is always involved, directly or indirectly, in the editing of a compilation. Sincere thanks to my wife Kaveeta for her immense support in all my academic pursuit as usual. I also wish to thank my sons Sushruta and Samrat, daughter-in-law Surovee, and granddaughter Shinjinee for their understanding. I record special thanks to my junior colleagues Dr. Dali Dutta and Dr. Juri Borah who volunteered for going through the typescript of the volume, and for helping me to detect and remove some typing errors.

Last, but not the least, a word of appreciation is also due to M/S Gyan Publishing House, New Delhi and their entire Staff members for their eagerness and sincere efforts toward bringing out the compilation within the stipulated time.

19 October 2018 **Sarthak Sengupta**

[illegible]

[illegible]

[illegible]

[illegible]

[illegible]

List of Tables

List of Contributors

Akhuan Gangmei Rongmei, Department of Anthropology, Manipur University, Chanchipur, Imphal, 795 003, Manipur.

Chandana Bhattacharjee, Department of Anthropology, Women's College, Shillong, 793003, Meghalaya.

Chandrajyoti Sonowal, Centre for Study of Social Inclusion and Inclusive Policies, Tata Institute of Social Sciences, Deonar, 400088, Mumbai.

Chura Giri, Department of Sociology, Margherita College, Margherita,

L. Doungel, Department of Political Science, D.H.S.K. College, Dibrugarh, 786 001, Assam.

M. C. Arunkumar, Department of Anthropology, Manipur University, Chanchipur, Imphal, 795 003, Manipur.

N. B. Biswas, Department of Education, Assam (Central) University, Silchar, 788011, Assam.

N. R. Roy, Department of Education, Assam (Central) University, Silchar, 788011, Assam.

Pushpa Champia, Centre for Juridical Studies, Dibrugarh University, Dibrugarh, 786 004, Assam.

Rudraman Thapa, Department of Political Science, Dibrugarh University, Dibrugarh, 786 004, Assam.

S. K. Chaudhuri, Indira Gandhi, Rashtriya Manav Sangrahalaya, Shamla Hills, Bhopal,

Sougaijam Priyokumar Meitei, Department of Anthropology, Manipur University, Chanchipur, Imphal, 795 003, Manipur.

Surajit Kumar Pal, Shivam Kunj, Nalini Apartment – 5, Flat No. F-1, Barde Nagar, Borgaon (East), Gorewara Rank Road, Nagpur, 440013, Maharashtra.

Surajit Sen, Department of English, Women's College, Shillong, 793003, Meghalaya.

Tarun Mene, Arunachal Pradesh of Tribal Studies, Rajiv Gandhi University, Rono Hilla, Itanagar, Papum Pare, 791112, Arunachal Pradesh.

CHAPTER - 1

SOCIAL MOVEMENTS: CONCEPTS, GENESIS, THEORIES AND SOME INSTANCES

CHANDRAJYOTI SONOWAL

Introduction

The term 'Social Movement' was introduced in 1850 by the German Sociologist Lorenz von Stein in his book '*History of French Social Movement from 1789 to the Present*' (1850). But the subject matter gained momentum in social sciences, especially sociologists, by the early part of 1960. Till then it was a domain of history and to some extent of political scientists.

The study of social movements had not remained a smooth sailing discourse for scholars for several reasons. The first and the foremost problems encountered by scholars were to define a 'social movement' bearing a universal acceptance. Though scholars' opinions vary, based on some components a social movement can be defined as 'a sustained collective mobilization through either formal or informal organizations having a sense of belonging and solidarity among members of the group involved in, launched with a special end or goal (Rudolph, 1951; Lewis, 1964; Rao, 2008)'.

Scholars also view social movements as an orientation towards a change of certain kind or sometimes resistance to changing aspects. Scholars like Rao (2008) argue that 'ideology' is an important component of social movements. It is because, without an ideology, a collective mobilization becomes individual or isolated event though it may have a change of orientation and collective mobilization. Lack of ideology makes it as a non-movement. But ideology may become a routine of a well established political party in an institutionalized form where the collective mobilization ceased to be a social movement.

There is a problem of classification of social movements as well. Scholars utilize different criteria to classify the social movements they study. Aberle (1966) describes four types of social movements based on two characters: (i) who is the movement attempting to change, and (ii) how much change is being advocated. This may be illustrated as follows:

		HOW MUCH CHANGE?	
		Limited A	Radical B
WHO IS CHANGED?	Specific Individual A	Alternative Social Movements AA	Redemptive Social Movements AB
	Every one B	Reformative Social Movements BA	Revolutionary Social Movements BB

Classification of Social Movements

On the basis of certain components involved in social movements across the world, social scientists have classified them into several categories. The Table 1.1 tries to illustrate them as follows:

Table 1.1. Classification of Social Movements

Classification of Social Movements		
Criteria	***Sub-Type***	***Example/Characteristics***
Scope/Consequences	Reform Movements	Aiming at changing legal norms, customs, and moral norms, methods may be reformist or radical
	Radical Movements	Aiming at fundamental changes in the value system
Types of Change	Innovation Movements	Want to enable new/refined norms, values etc.
	Conservative Movements	Want to preserve existing norms and values etc.
Targets	Group focus movements	Focused on affecting groups or society in general (e.g., change of political system).
	Individual-focus movements	Focused on affecting individuals like religious movements
Methods of Work	Peaceful movements	Peacefully accomplished like the American Civil Rights Movements, Polish Solidarity Movements
	Violent Movements	Various armed movements across the world
Old and New	Old Movements	Movements for specific social groups like working class, peasants, Blacks, political autonomy etc.
	New Movements	Feminist movements, Environmental movements, Gay rights etc.
Range (Scale and Spatial spread	Global movements	Movements for global civil society, Universal Human Rights etc
	Local Movements	Most of the social movements are of a local type
	Multi-level movements	A movement that recognizes the complexity of governance in the 21st century and aims to have an impact at the local, regional, national and international levels.
Locus	Subjective	Tribal movements, Caste movements, Peasants movements, ethnic movements etc.
	Objective	Linguistic, Feministic, religious etc.

The classification of movements helps to identify the name features of a movement. To understand the origin, growth, dynamics and consequences one has to rely on other components of movements. Scholars also point out that all such classifications are relative to the specific phase of development of the movement because movements tend to acquire new features during its course.

The Genesis of Social Movements

Traditional Theories: One of the main issues in the study of any movement is the concerns about its emergence. In conceptualizing the genesis of any movement few points have to be concerned, namely, (i) the structural conditions under which movements emerge, (ii) the motivational force that leads to movement, (iii) the theories that conceptualize the genesis of movement and (iii) adequacy of theories to explain all these aspects.

Broadly speaking, there are three traditional basic theories which try to explain the emergence of social movements, namely, (i) theories of relative deprivation, (ii) structural strain theory (iii) revitalization theory.

New Social Movements

The social movements in contemporary societies have shown some categorical difference from previous or old social movements. Thus, studying these new social movements are basically conceptualized under two dominant theoretical paradigms.

From the 1950s and 1970s onwards, the US and Europe saw a surge of protests and demonstration against government policies and social conventions. The people involved in these protests often cut across class, division and the issues involved anti-nuclear, anti-armament, women's movements, lifestyle etc. As against the breakdown theories of existing paradigm, the new situation demands a new theoretical base to analyze new types of collective mobilization. This has brought up a new paradigm called the *Resource Mobilization Theory.* This theory focused not on why the movements take place, but on

Table 1.2. Traditional Theories of Social Movement

Broad theory	***Subtype***	***Basic premises/ aspects***
Relative deprivation theory	Social mobility	People are driven by movements out of a sense of deprivation or inequality, particularly; *In relation to others*: Participants see others who have more power, economic resources or status and thus try to acquire these things for themselves. *In relation to their expectations*: People are most likely to rebel when a consistently improving situation stops and makes a turn for worse. People's expectations exceed the actual material situation and the revolt.
	Social conflict	Marx and Aberle developed the concept of relative deprivation emphasizing the element of conflict. Marxism arose from an analysis of movements structured by conflicts between industrial workers and their employers in the 19th century. Marx and Engels (1973) recognized that dissatisfaction with the status quo was not determined by absolute conditions but by relative expectations. Aberle (1966) defined relative deprivation as a negative discrepancy between legitimate expectations and actuality. For him, relative deprivation may surface in material possession, status, behaviour, and worth.
Structural strain theory (Smelser, 1962)	Structural conduciveness	People come to believe their society has problems.
	Structural strain:	People experience deprivation.
	Growth and spread of a solution	A solution to the problems people are experiencing is proposed and spread.
	Precipitating factors:	Discontent usually requires a catalyst (often a specific event) to turn it into a social movement.
	Lack of social control:	The entity that is to be changed must be at least somewhat open to the change (if quickly and powerfully repressed it fails).
	Mobilization:	This is the actual organizing an active component of the movement: people do what needs to be done.
Revitalization theory	Period of cultural stability.	Wallace (1956) opines that social movements develop out of a deliberate, organized and conscious effort on the part of members of a society to construct a more satisfying culture for themselves. Under the four stages of dynamics of revitalization movement one can see the following reactions: Express dissatisfaction, dissent, and protest against existing conditions. Offer a positive program of action to remedy the situation.
	Period of increased individual stress.	
	Period of cultural distortion and consequent disillusionment	
	Period of revitalization.	

how the movement is organized and why some of them were more successful than the others. A variant of the theory which focuses on the political rather than on civil society realm is the political process approach. It sees social movements as a form of mass politics.

Western European social scientists deliberated these issues a little later, by 1970s. They asserted that present-day collective action is not confined to negotiation and strategic calculation by social movements to gain political power. Rather the movements involve issues of social norms and identity, and the struggle takes place in the realm of civil society rather than in the realm of politics. The theoretical paradigm thus developed is called New Social Movement Theory (NSM). In general, the NSM approach explains the social movements as linked to the failure of the democratic system in the post-modern society to guarantee individual freedom, equality, and fraternity.

These theories argue that democracy is degenerating into an authoritarian, technocratic state. The state, in turn, has become subjugated to market forces. People are thus dominated by the state's technocracy and the forces of the market. There are no longer workers but are consumers. The old class of workers has ceased to be a class in the production process. Instead, people's main social role has become that of consumers. In this role, they are entirely manipulated by the market.

For Touraine (1995) the state, the market and the domain of communication and media are gradually diminishing the liberty of the individuals. The expanding structures of state and market economy along with mass media advance colonize the public and private sphere of individuals, which Habermas (1981) calls the life-world. This life-world includes the domains in which meaning and values reside – such as family, education, art, religion. So, private life becomes steadily more politicized by this double encroachment.

Thus, social movements are seen as defensive reactions to defend the public and the private spheres of individuals against the inroads of the state system and market economy.

Participation in social movements is the only way in which the individual can recover liberty. The main role of social movements is the mobilization of 'actors/subjects' (individuals) in their full role as free and creative members of a pluralistic society, as opposed to victims or objects of state and market domain.

The New Social Movement approach emphasizes the cultural nature of the new movements and views them as a struggle for control over the production of meaning and the constitution of new collective identities. It stresses the expressive aspects of social movements and places them exclusively in the terrain of civil society, as opposed to the state. This approach also emphasizes discontinuity by highlighting the differences between the new movements and traditional collective actors.

Resource mobilization theory, in contrast, stresses that political nature of the new movements and interprets them as conflicts over the allocation of goods in the political market. Hence it focuses on the strategic-instrumental aspects of action and places social movements, simultaneously, at the level of civil society and the state. It also places 6emphasis on the continuity between the new and the old collective actors.

These theories can be summarized in tabular form as follows:

Table 1.3. Modern Theories of Social Movement

Theories	*Types of resources*	*Basic premises*
Resource mobilization theory	Material	Money and physical capital
	Moral	Solidarity, support for the movement's goal.
	Social organization	Organizational strategies, social networks, bloc recruitment
	Human	Volunteers, staff, leaders
	Cultural	Prior activist experience, understanding the issues, collective actions, know-how.

(Contd...)

Political process theory	Increase access to political decision-making power.	Certain political contexts should be conducive (or representative) for a potential social movement activity. Political opportunity is the central requirement of social movement in this theory.
	Instability in the alignment of ruling elites (or conflicts between elites).	
	Access to elite allies (who can then help a movement in its struggle).	
	Declining capacity and propensity of the state to repress dissent.	

Culture Theory

Another variant of New Social Movement approach is the Culture Theory. It builds upon both the political process and resource mobilization theories but extends them in two ways: first, it emphasizes the importance of movement culture. Second, it attempts to address the free-rider problem. Culture theory brings the 'sense of injustice' present in resource mobilization and political process theory to the forefront of movement created by arguing that in order for social movements to successfully mobilize individuals, they must develop an 'injustice frame'. An Injustice Frame is a collection of ideas and symbols that illustrate both how significant the problem is as well as what the movement can do to alleviate it.

In emphasizing the injustice frame, culture theory also addresses the free rider problem. It refers to the idea that people will not be motivated to participate in a social movement that will use up their personal resources (e.g. time, money, etc.) if they can still receive the benefits without participating. A significant problem for social movement theory has been to explain why people join movements if they believe the movement can/will succeed without their contribution. Culture theory argues that, in conjunction with social network being an important contact tool, the injustice frame will provide the motivation for people to contribute to the movement.

Framing processes include three separate components:

1. Diagnostic frame: The movement organization frames what is the problem or what they are critiquing.
2. Prognostic Frame: The movement organization frames what is the desirable solution to the problems.
3. Motivational Frame: The movement organization frames a 'Call to Arms' by suggesting and encouraging that people take action to solve the problem.

Collective human behaviour approach yet another paradigm the '*Collective human behaviour*' approach considers as a normal state of society the stable functioning of an unchanging society. This approach can be very useful during the period when society is unambiguously at a stable state of its development. The Resource Mobilization approach considers as normal permanent stable development with constant small social changes but it ignores the possibility that society can be stable at definite stages. The NSM approach and action-identity approach take into consideration both the moments of development (transition from industrial to post-industrial society) and the moment of stability.

Some Reflection on Main Causes of Social Movements

Next point to be considered is the main cause of the emergence of social movements and their essence. RM approaches think that the SM is the form of adaptation and accommodation of society that is the natural moment of development, as a reaction to changes, of a society without sharp contradictions. The 'collective behaviour' approach connects the emergence of social movements with conflicts. When the society is healthy, it has no contradiction and all activity is channeled through conventional forms. The exponents of the 'action-identity' approach stress the normal nature of social movements, but sharp contradictions exist always as the expression of different class interests. The NSM and 'new value approach' do not connect the emergence and activity of social movements either with conflicts or with the absence of conflicts. They stress the possibility of both cases, although the 'new social movements' is closer to the explanation of conflicts as a manifestation of social contradiction and the 'New Value' approach is closer to the opposite points of views.

Some of the basic premises of emergence of social movements are:

1. They are likely to evolve when the time and the place are friendly.
2. Emerge in different forms in liberal and authoritarian societies.
3. There must always be polarizing differences between groups of people. In the case of old movements, they were the poverty and wealth gap. In the case of new movements, they are most likely to be the difference in customs, ethics, and values.
4. It needs an initiating event: a particular, individual event that will begin a chain reaction of events in the given society leading to the creation of a social movement.

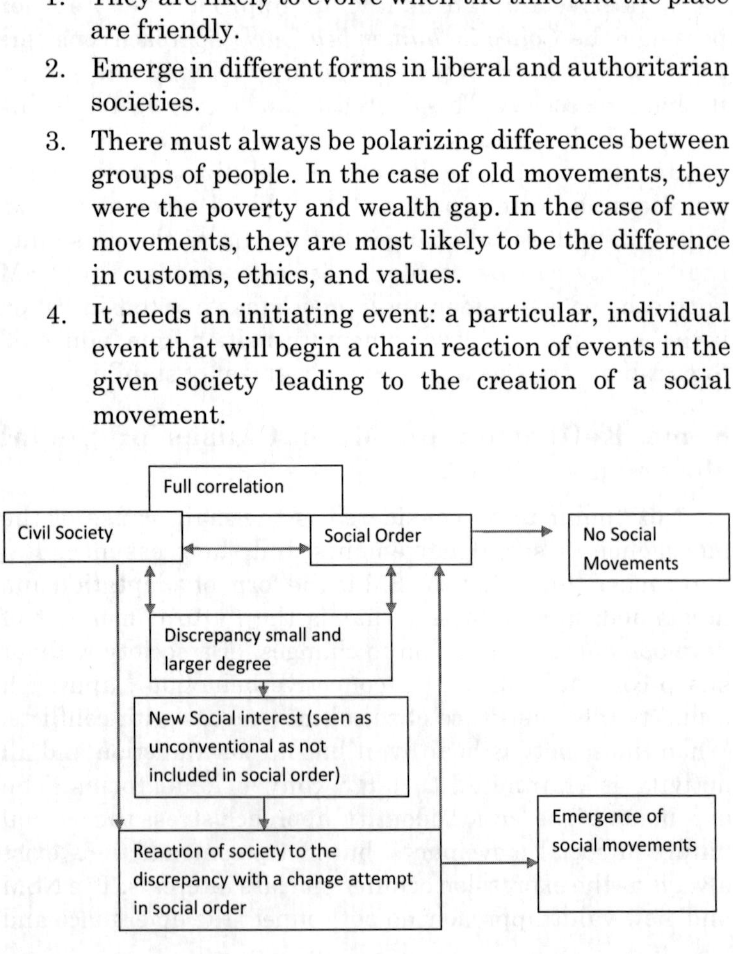

- Social interests are social forces in one sense and when they do not get the opportunity to express adequately in social order movements occur aiming at changing the social order to accommodate these interests. Larger the discrepancy stronger the Social movements, and smaller the discrepancy weaker the social movements or conventional in nature.
- Main social interest in a particular society depends on
    - (i) Stages of development of the society
    - (ii) Characteristics of the civil society
- Interests may be hierarchical

Stages of Social Movements

Social movements are not eternal. They have a life cycle: they are created, they grow, they achieve success or failure and eventually, they dissolve and cease to exist. Blumer (1969), Mauss (1975), and Tilly (1978) have described different stages social movements often pass through. Movements emerge for a variety of reasons, coalesce, and generally bureaucratize. At that point, they can take a number of paths, including finding some form of movement success, failure, co-optation of leaders, repression by larger groups (e.g., government), or even the establishment of the movement within the mainstream.

Whether these paths will result in movement decline or not varies from movement to movement. In fact, one of the

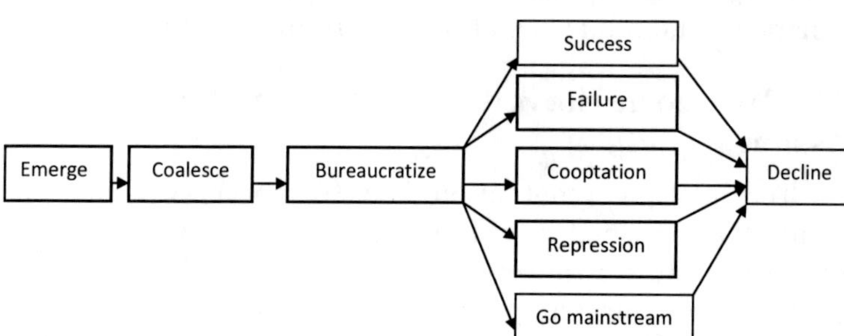

difficulties in studying social movements is that movement success is often ill-defined because movement goals can change.

Social Movements in Northeast India

Northeast India has been experiencing varied nature and quantum of movements from historical past. While most of its movements are political in its orientation there are some other movements that are development related and socio-economic in nature. It is true that we cannot deny the political underpinning of most of the movements in the region. Much has been written and documented about different movements in the region. Thus, the aim of the present section of the chapter is to find out some not so widely talked about aspects of some movements in Assam.

To fulfill the aim of the chapter some events of social movements have been picked up for delineation. From the conventional history of Assam, the famous Moamoria movement has been picked up to show how conventional history keeps itself away from analytical aspects and depicts an oversimplified and sometimes deliberately manufactured picture of our past. Second, the event of peasant movement and the incidence of Patharughat (which will be described subsequently) have been taken for a quick look. Finally, the tribal movements against the dominance of a conceptually created identity called Assamese during the dawn of independence and its consequences till date, which have never come up with popular literature or history of Assam or Northeast India has been taken for re-interpretation.

The Moamoria[1] Revolt as the Peasant Movement in Assam

Terminological contention: The Moamoria revolt has been generally described as a religious revolt against the royal atrocity faced by the religious leaders and dignitaries of Moamoria religion in upper Assam. An analysis of the socio-political and socio-economic situation of those days and the nature and extent of participation of people in it clearly reveals that it was a peasant movement guided by dignitaries of Moamoria (Mayamora) Satras[2]

The Underlying Factors

Deprivation and Exploitation under Royal domain: Exploitation of human resources and exploitation of labour was quite evident during the Ahom[3] rule which became very organized before the revolt. It was usually done by *Pyke* system where every able adult member of a family was designated as a *Pyke*. Four such *Pykes* were grouped together to form a '*Goot*'. One of the members of the '*goot*' had to work or render physical services for royal interest alternately for three months in a year while other three looked after his family in needs. *Pykes* used to get a very limited arable land to cultivate which were not permanently owned by them. There was also rule to construct and deconstruct '*goots*' to avoid group solidarity among the pykes. Besides physical labour, the *pykes* had to pay a part of their produce as taxes of a different kind to the royal administration. *Pykes* were distributed to different royal officers and families and these royal officials had absolute authority on the *pykes*. Due to increased demand, the '*goots*' were formed by three *pykes* later on, ultimately increasing the duration of compulsory service to royal interest from three months to four months a year by every *pyke*. The *pykes* did not have freedom. They had to move where the needs of royal interest emerged. Their labour was unpaid one like slaves. Thus we see a double burden of exploitation on the *pykes* of Ahom age.

Relative freedom under Satras: The religious bodies were also granted with lots of land and *pykes* free of taxes. Such *pykes* were exempted from working for royal interest. They had to work to make temples and religious establishments. They had to pay religious taxes to the Satra. But they were allowed to cultivate in the vast area of land available under the Satra. In due course of time, they transformed from landed slaves to free *ryots*[4]. They were converted to Vaishnavism and became economically independent farmers.

Vaishnavism, as we know, flourished in Assam under the able leadership of Sri Sankardeva. It could attract a lot of local people immediately due to its liberal philosophy. Few scholars observe the feudal characteristics in Vaishnava Satra arrangement. This was because of the doctrine of Bhakti; the ultimate ideology of Vaishnavism is the unflinching loyalty to God. The very notion submitted by a Vaishnava novice is – '*me, slave of the slave of thy*'. This notion had strengthened the feudalism in the form of Satra organization along with the royal administration arrangement. There may be a difference of terminology of taxes and services, but the common men were exploited the same way. What important was that a parallel feudalism to royal domain emerged in the form of Satra Institution during Ahom rule. In some cases, the Satra and the Royal Ahom administration were complementing each other in needs.

The life within Satra arrangement for common men was lucrative because those people were free from compulsory service and taxes to royal interest. Also, they had economic independence to a greater extent. Moreover, they had a better social and religious life under the Satra's liberal policy. These were the reasons for which thousands of *pykes* used to enter into *Satra* domain.

Conflict of interest between Royal Court and Satras: Increase of power of Satra institution through its *ryots* and followers was a matter of concern for the Royal court. Thus some of the Satra institutions were lured towards Royal court by offering royal privileges. Satras under royal patronage were established. But the emerging power of Satras was irresistible. For obvious political and economic reason, the Satras were attacked by the Ahom kings.

Ahom king Godadhar Singha (1681-1695) started, for the first time, an organized attack on satras following a mass exodus of *pykes* from royal domain towards Satra domain taking the advantage of political instability before him. As a measure of capturing runaway *pykes,* he first drove away from the married novices from the Satra domain. After that, he drove away all the Vaishnavite novices other than the Brahmins, Kayastha, Mahanta, and Kalitas. All other unmarried novices were categorized as '*Dhod*' (lazy and worthless) and were compelled to work in infrastructure development like building roads and digging ponds etc. The famous road called '*Dhodor Ali*' (road made by *Dhod*) was constructed by such Vaishnavite novices.

It is to be noted that while several Satra institutions were divided on the basis of caste, rituals, purity etc after Sankardeva and Madhabdeva, the Moamoria Satras in upper Assam were free from such classification and in due course of time it emerged as a superior power center.

Atrocities on common people: As royal atrocity on common people increased, people's dissatisfaction against royal administration was also increased. Namghar[5] and Satras became a meeting point and seminal ground for political and socio-economic aspects of common people. To hide from the eyes of royal spies (*churangchua*) people created some secret rituals in the name of religion where only selected adults were allowed to participate. Such secret societies are still prevalent among the Moamoria societies.

Satras as Leadership base: The base of the public support towards Moamoria Satra was so strong that even after the repeated destruction of Satras by the Royal forces; those were rebuilt immediately by the novices. It is recorded that following a huge assembly of Moamoria novices to build a '*Bor-Namghar* (Big or Main Monastery) in Malow Ali of Jorhat district, the leaders of Vaishnavite novices insisted to revolt against Ahom king and capture him. But due to hesitant Satradhikar, it could not be materialized.

That the Moamoria Mahantas did not represent the causes of their common novices, and that they exhibited typical feudalistic mentality, was quite evident while they were initially reluctant to lead the revolt against the Ahom king. It is said that the eldest son of Moamoria Mahanta, Gagini or Bayan Deka, who wanted to lead the revolt against Ahom king, was advised by his father as follows:

> ' ..... *why do you need royal treasure, you, who have the uncountable amount of gold and silver, half of the country's public as novices making us equal to the king, ten to twelve thousand dedicated novices, eight to ten thousand slaves, ten to twelve estates, thousands of cattle.*' In the same way, he also advised his son that '*small revolute only change its courses, but a sea never changes its place. When a sea changes its place a country gets destroyed,...... though an enemy should be inflicted pain, it is the king who will bear the pain, and the king is our father*'.

These delineations clearly suggest that the Moamoria Mahanta was a kind of great feudal lord and his stand as a specific class member was quite evident. He was quite sure that waging war against the king would have meant a great loss to him also. It was the tremendous pressure of the novices which compelled the Moamoria Mahanta to lead the revolt against the Ahom king.

Torture on Moamoria religious dignitaries by the royal administration was quite evident over a period of time. Nityananda Deva was murdered in 1650, Baikunthanath Deva was killed in 1694, Chaturbhoja Deva was demoralized in 1704, and he was sentenced to death during the reign of King Siva Singha and Queen Phuleswari Kunwari. It was seen that those Moamoria novices were hurt by such killings. But they did not outburst till their local leaders were tortured and killed. It was quite widely spoken that Moamoria revolt emerged as a result of conflicts between Sakta[6]and Vaishnava religious dignitaries and due to the torture of Vaishnava gurus at the behest of Sakta religious dignitaries.

Usually, the Brahmin communities propagated Saktaism (following Sakta way of religion) in Assam. They did not have mass followers like the Vaishnavism. They were basically dependent on royal supports. Obviously, they always tried to initiate the king and his royal families and officers to Saktaism. Saktaism flourished during the reign of Siva Singha when Saktaism was established as a Royal religion. The inherent caste division also flourished along with the Saktaism and it got translated among the different royal families and the gap widened between rulers and the ruled. Tantrik[7] guru Krishnakanta Nyayabagish (Parbotiya Gohain) who was brought from Bengal by Ahom king Rudra Singha became so powerful in the royal court that he was able to convince the king Siva Singha to leave his crown to his wife Phuleswari kunwari and thus dominated by the royal decisions.

These Sakta Brahmins always insisted kings to take action against Vaishnava gurus, especially against the Mayamara Satra. While the Sakta gurus had limited followers including the king and royal families and officers, Vaishnava gurus had a huge public base. This status quo of *pyke* system was a need for such Sakta religious fraternity and to several other Vaishnavite Satras which depended on royal patronage and labour of free *pykes*. For obvious reason, this group of religious fraternity stood by the Ahom king during Moamoria revolt.

Dominant Interest and Fabrication of History: Literature available on this revolt usually depicts the one-sided or partial picture of the entire event. It very skilfully shades a curtain on another side of the revolt, the exploitation of labour and resources, oppression of common people under *pyke* system and burden of taxes, the slave system, and land relation, economic stagnation, and lack of freedom of common people. This mass revolt was nothing but a spontaneous expression of hatred and dissatisfaction against the widespread and systematic oppression and exploitation of common people, unbearable slavery and torture current in those days.

In the struggle against organized odds, we can see the role of religion as the organizing or unification agent all over the world. Thus, though several mass revolts in medieval age look like religious revolt, in fact, those were the reflection of class conflicts between the rulers and the ruled, between oppressors and the oppressed. It is also seen that many a time leaders of such revolts emerge from the feudal classes who for their own interests lead the outburst of oppressed masses. As mentioned in the stages of the struggle, usually such leaders hesitate to take straight or firm steps in the course of the struggle. Sometimes they take the struggle to reform movement, sometimes get eliminated for being unable to provide suitable leadership.

Land Regulation and Peasant Movement during British Period: The incidence of Patharughat of Mongoldoi is remembered as a mark of the earliest known peasant movement in Assam. But very little has been written about the background factors and the course of the movement. The incidence of Pathorughat was intimately related to the expansion of tea industry in Assam.

Capitalist Interest: The Assam Tea Company was started in 1839. By 1857 there emerged 51 tea estates in Assam. Faced with an acute labour shortage the planters community urged the government in 1859 to further enhance the land revenue rates so that the poor peasants could be flushed out of their villages to work for wages on the plantations. They also recommended putting a ban on the cultivation and sale of local opium

Accordingly, the government increased the land revenue rates 15 to 30 percent of dry crops land. It also placed a ban on the cultivation of poppy in 1860 but opened the market for the sale of opium from north India and the price of opium was increased to double. It hit hard to local peasant as poppy was the only assured means of cash income. The increased price also made them prone to the net of money lenders. The land revenue was further increased on both dry and wet rice land to double arbitrarily.

It was a situation which Dr. Amalendu Guha describes as 'Rob the peasant to pay Planters'. In 1843 colonial government abolished the slavery system or the *pyke* system under which the common people were rendering services to the Ahom aristocracy, Brahmins, Mahantas and such other landowners. An estimate shows that nearly 5 to 9 percent of the population was acted as bonded slavery under this system. But such release from slavery was not followed by any rehabilitation programme. They simply became tenants under landowners.

The discriminating land revenue rate determined for tea planters and local peasants was evident from the following illustration:

Table 1.4. Wasteland Settlement Rules 1838 and 1854

Rules of 6 March 1838				*Rules of 23 October 1854 irrespective of Categories of Land used*	
Three categories of Wasteland			*Land Revenue per acre*	*Time Periods*	*Land Revenue per Acre*
Under Grass	*Under Reeds and High Gras*	*Under Forests*			
1st 5 years	1st 10 years	1st 20 years	Nil	1st 15 years	Nil
Next 6-8 years	11-13 years	21-23 years	9 *annas*	18-25 years	3 *annas*
Next 8-30 years	14-35 years	24-35 years	Rs. 1-2 *annas*	26-99 years	6 *annas*
On expiry of Lease			At par with Rice lands	On expiry of Lease	At par with Rice lands
One-fourth of grants perpetually Revenue Free				One-fourth of grants perpetually Revenue Free	

Source: Baden-Powel, 1895, pp. 410-414.

This table shows that while the peasants paid Rs 3 to Rs. 1-8 as per acre of their land holding in 1870, the planters paid nothing at all for the major part of their land holding.

It was under the settlement rules of 1870 that the government, for the first time, recognized the permanent, transferable and heritable rights in *rupit* (wet paddy) and *bari* (homestead) land in private occupation.

Under the 1870 Rules, wet paddy and homestead lands were settled for a period of ten years at fixed rates, subject to a revision at the end of the period. From 1883, however, the settlement made for this category of land was invariably decennial. Other categories of land suitable for dry crops continued to be settled on an annual basis since the relevant cultivation was of a shifting nature. There were not vested with permanent, transferable rights and could be taken back by the government for public purposes without any compensation. The *ryot* continued to have the option of relinquishing any amount of land under either category, at own convenience.

The economic condition of the peasantry in 1880 was under prosperous despite the increased demand for farm products from plantation and railway construction activities. The numbers of money lenders were 1,793 in Brahmaputra valley according to 1891 census and most of them were concentrated in Kamrup district alone. But the insignificant presence of money lenders does not reveal that there was no indebtedness among the peasants of Assam proper. Because the market sector of the peasant economy has been completely in the grip of the well-entrenched Marwari[8] trading capital ever since the advent of the British rule. Peasants used to receive cash advances from the Marwari traders against pledged crops to a considerable extent. The census put these traders and their agents mostly under the category of petty shopkeepers, rather than moneylenders.

Inquiries made in 1882-1983 suggested that there were only a few under-tenants, except on the partially or wholly revenue free estates of Kamrup. The extent of tenancy in the wholly revenue free land was widespread. Such tenants did not enjoy occupancy rights anywhere in the Brahmaputra valley. The settlement statistics of 1893 revealed that in Kamrup *mauza* as much as one-third of the settled area was sub-let. In south Kamrup, this proportion was one-fifth. The land record shows that the accumulation of leases was in the hands of non-cultivators who were mostly government office clerks, and pleaders of district towns who had a command over ready money. Not many of the non-cultivating landowners were Marwari merchants. This was because they were more interested in seizing the crop for settlement of an advance than in seizing the land. Hence, Marwaris did not feature as an important absentee landholding group.

Resentment to enhanced land revenue: The impending enhancement of land revenue rates under the new settlement, as notified in 1892, led to a widespread dissatisfaction that rocked the rural society. The *ryot*s complained that because they had to pay the government an exorbitant price for opium, they were unable to pay the enhanced land revenue. The Sarvajanik Sabha of Jorhat held a series of meetings from October 1892 to February 1893, to protest against the government policy of an 'excessive increase of revenue'.

Under the new settlement, the population density and the demand for land in each village were the chief consideration in determining the land value and the rate to be fixed. The revised rates in the Brahmaputra[9] valley initially involved an enhancement of 53 percent on average, but in many villages, it was as high as 70 to 100 percent. Though it was reduced to 37 percent, later on, the *ryots* demanded a postponement of the collection even at the reduced rate until the final orders of the Government of India on the pending appeal were received. People in Kamrup and central Assam spontaneously organized themselves once more into specially convened local *mels*[10] to decide upon a no-rent campaign.

In these *mels,* the *ryots* discussed the increasing economic burden on them. They were already paying the much higher price for opium – a government monopoly. Year after year they had been pledging their crops to Marwari traders to get advances for paying the land revenue. Now the demand for enhanced land revenue would push them further into the grip of usurious capital. Thus, caught in a vicious circle of intensified exploitation, they started agitating not only against the government but also against the Marwari traders. *Mels* were held throughout December and January 1893 in all *mauzas*[11] of North Kamrup. Everywhere the *mels* directed people not to pay the enhanced rates. Thousands of people demonstrated in and around Rangiya for several days. Armed police and military forces were posted at several places to stop the demonstration. Several incidences of the arrest of leaders and forceful release of them by demonstrators were reported in several places. The government found it difficult to collect land revenue in the *tahsils* of Patidarang, Nalbari, Barama, and Bajali and in the *mauza* of Upar Barbhag and Sarukhetri – all forming a compact block.

Suppressive measures: Meanwhile a reign of terror was let loose. Notices were served on principal headmen of the area, under Section 17 of Act V of 1861, to act as special constables for the preservation of peace. The *ryots* were told by the *Raj* (government): 'if you do not pay, your property will be attached.' The *raij* (the common people) told him: 'If you do pay, you will be cursed and excommunicated.' The people were further directed by the *raij* not to bid for the purchase of attached properties put on auction. Disobedience was threatened with social boycott and excommunication, as well as the imposition of fines.

All licensed guns in Rangiya, Nalbari, Barama and Bajali tahsils were seized. Respectable citizens over the entire affected area were forced into the special constabulary. On 21 January 1894, a group of *ryots* assaulted the *mouzadar* and *mandal* when they tried to collect revenue at Kapla near Lachima in Sarukhetri *mauza*. Seventy-five persons arrested by the police were released by 3000 strong assemblies of people. By 25 January, 59 principal leaders were arrested and forced to construct a makeshift lockup for themselves. The same evening about 6000 people approached the District Magistrate's camp and presented a mass petition, signed by all of them, for the release of those arrested. They finally dispersed after a bayonet charge was ordered.

The most tragic incident took place at Patharughat in Mongoldoi subdivision, on 28th January 1894. Thousands of people had rallied in anticipation of the arrival of District Magistrate of Darrang to demand retreat of land revenue hike. They refused to disperse unless their demands were met. A bayonet charge and volleys of firing followed, causing the deaths, according to official reports, of fifteen *ryots* and injury to as many as thirty-six. The *ryots* also answered by throwing clods of earth and bamboo sticks. In front of such necked attack, the movements could not be continued. Villagers were tortured and their properties destroyed or looted. The people were forced to pay the enhanced revenue.

The widespread peasant struggle, based on the unity of the entire peasantry and a section of the non-cultivating landowners, made an impact on the contemporary Assamese society. The non-cultivation land owners – Brahmins, Mahantas and Dolois, the traditional rural elite—apparently took the initiatives and a leading role in the struggle. But it was the poor peasantry and other section of the rural poor, including the artisans, who lent it a militant character. One of the militant artisans, Pusparam Kanhar, is still remembered, *inter alias*, by the bell-metal workers of Saruhetri *mauza* as having undergone a term of imprisonment.

It may be noted that in the disturbed *mauzas* and *tahsils*, tenants constituted a large proportion of the population and occupied so one-third of the settled area. The land-owners apprehended that it would be difficult to shift their burden of the enhancement in land revenue rates on to the shoulders of their tenants. They feared that their profits as middlemen would, therefore, be cut down. This consideration pushed them into the agitation. But, afraid of the loss of property under attachment orders, they did not continue their resistance for long. Indeed they were the first to retreat.

Political Assertions of Tribal Groups in Assam

A flawless description of the genesis of ethnic assertion

in Assam is hard to forward due to lack of authentic record of diverse issues raised at the different point of time. Some of the available documents published so far are said to be truncated in nature affecting the total truth.

Amidst the scarcity of record, the formation of 'Assam Plains Tribal League' in 1933 can be counted as the dawn of political assertion of ethnic groups in Assam. It was an epoch-making event in the sense that during that period the 'Assam Franchise Committee' which was formed in 1932 was reviewing the proposed electoral policy and different aspects on the formation of 'Assam Legislative Assembly' and 'Assam Legislative Council' to be incorporated in upcoming '1935 Government of India Act.'. The 'Assam Franchise Committee' was planning to consider only the Bodo Kacharis, the Mech, the Lalungs (Tiwa) and the Miri (Mishing) as backward classes of Assam and to grant separate reservation to them. Considering such a situation along with those four communities, the other backward ethnic groups also planned to unite together to create a 'pressure group' to take constitutional advantage by entering into reserved and special categories. These populations did not get any such special treatment according to 1919 Government of India Act through these groups appealed for the same at individual capacity. In its first meet held in Roha, the newly formed 'Assam Plains Tribal League' proposed to demand the government to treat those groups together as one entity rather than separately and reserve at least seven seats in Assam Legislative Assembly. As a result, they got four reserved seats.

The assertion of these backward communities was not a smooth journey. Their prudent movements were labeled as anti-national (against Assamese nationality) by different thinkers and intellectuals. It was propagated that the Tribal League decided to advise the backward class people to denote themselves by their ethnic identity in ensuing 1941 census as instigated by Saadulla. Contrary to such speculation, in treaty signed with Saadulla's United Muslim Party on 16-3-1940 the precondition (No. 4 in the first one and No. 7 in the second one) for supporting these two coalition governments were that irrespective of religious affiliation, backward ethnic groups would be recorded as 'Tribal' in ensuing 1941 general census. Late Jogendra Nath Hazarika, in fact, appealed along with other leaders of Tribal League not to fall into the trap of Saadulla's soft policy on immigrant Muslims and kept vigilance on political representatives on this issue. He also appealed people, following the census policy of Tribal League, to denote themselves by their tribe or ethnic names after stating their language as Assamese and religion, for example, Hindu Kachari, Hindu Deori, Christian Bodo etc. Kachari leaders like Dambarudhar Saikia, Mitharam Bora, Yadab Chandra Khaklari etc propagated this policy in such a magnitude that even the Kachari novices, who had been Vaishnavite for several generations did not hesitate to enter their identity as tribals. Thus, the number of tribal people increased to 28, 24,133 from its previous number of 12, 39,280 according to 1911 census. Newspapers like Asom, Assam Tribune, etc doctored and truncated the statement of tribal leaders to weaken tribal organizations and there was hardly any difference of opinion between Caste Hindu Assamese middle class and Congress leaders.

The common assumption among the so-called nationalist Assamese, regarding the assertion of backward communities, was nothing but a conspiracy to destroy the greater national interest of a nation or a wider society. It was believed that some actors of vested interest, taking the advantage of perceived or felt discrimination of such ethnic groups, instigate them towards the movement. The thinking of many intellectuals forwarded the view that the ethnic assertions have the genesis in colonial divide and rule policy where the colonial administration used these ethnic groups as a tool to break the freedom struggle by making a separation of interest among them. The ethnic leaders, according to this proposition, are nothing more than puppets of colonial play. But the true fact is that a few of the people of these ethnic groups, taking the limited opportunity provided by the British, though for their colonial interest, educated themselves only to realize the situation of their own community and gradually develop the essence of self-determination which they lost on long historical intercourse. Another viewpoint says that the assertions of these backward ethnic groups are nothing but the conspiracy of a vested interest group who are against the Assamese nationalism. It says that some vested interest group instigate the ignorant and innocent tribal people to revolt or agitate to destroy the greater social web. Contrary to such views one can say that in the freedom struggle, several leaders of Tribal League participated wholeheartedly. During the 'grouping' of Assam, the Tribal League, along with other backward communities took a firm stand supporting Congress party's policy. Likewise, in the movement for language, refinery, foreigner's issue etc tribal students and youth took part impressively. Under Kalaguru Bishnuprasad Rabha, tribal people invariably took part in communist movement too. Thus, the assertion of backward ethnic groups was treated and presented negatively by the elite section. This trend continued in Assam till the late eighties of last century. Following the extreme magnitude of tribal movement, especially the Bodo movement, the elite group of Assam started treating the issues as a problem related to the core of tribal people's life ways.

Some leading thinkers among the tribal people of Assam feel that it was an irreparable mistake done by Congress government of Assam when they sent a tribal person as representative of tribal people of plains of Assam who was actually a loyal leader of Congress party and surely, did not represent and was not a recognized representative of tribal people. In 1946, in the month of July Congress sent 10 members to constituent Assembly for the formulation of Indian Constitution. Among them, Dharanidhar Basumatary was sent as a tribal representative who was a hardcore loyal congress member. Following the policy of Congress party, which was dominated by Caste-Hindu middle-class people and who perceived their own interest as the interest of the whole of Assam, did not like the idea of having special treatment and safeguard in the constitution for tribal people. Thus, the representative did not advocate for the protection of plains tribes under 5th or 6th schedule. But Rev. J.J.N. Roy was vocal for the cause of the hills people whom he represented too. Contrary to the indifference of Congress leaders towards tribal causes, the Tribal League sacrificed its demand for separate electorate for the sake of the retention of the greater Assamese identity.

It has already been mentioned that some of the tribal people got educated and had the exposure to the non-tribal domain. Eventually, some Bodo and Rabha people entered the military and para-military services. In due course of time, they became aware of the plight of their people and also created awareness in their society. But their formal appeal for due favour was not taken care of. Fed up with such deprivation these people started forming their organizations and started putting pressure on concerned authority collectively. Among the Bodos, Kalicharan Brahma, who was a forest contractor, took leading part. Under his auspices, Bodo Students Union was formed in 1915 in Dhubri. Then he formed the 'Bodo Mahasanmilon' in 1923. Till date their aspiration was non-political. But as college and university educated Bodo people emerged on the scene, they could observe the special benefits enjoyed by the high Caste Hindu Assamese of Brahmaputra valley and the Bengali people of Borak valley and also the Muslims for whom special benefits were provided by the Government of India Act, 1919 through the procedure of Diarchy (A system of double government introduced by the Government of India Act (1919) for the provinces of British India. It marked the first introduction of the democratic principle into the executive branch of the British administration of India. Though much-criticized, it signified a breakthrough in British Indian government and was the forerunner of India's full provincial autonomy (1935) and independence (1947). Dyarchy was introduced as a constitutional reform by Edwin Samuel Montagu (Secretary of State for India, 1917–22) and Lord Chelmsford (Viceroy of India, 1916–21).

Due to the absence of representatives from tribal and backward class people in the Reform Council, their appeals were not materialized. In this circumstance, Bodo people tried to elect their candidates to Reform Council but their candidate was defeated twice in a non-Muslim constituency in Dhubri. As the right of franchise was vested in holding of real and movable property, only a few tribal people had the right to vote, and they, too, were scattered over a large area. Seeing the impossibility of winning an election, the Bodos, while submitting their memorandum to Simon Commission in 1929, demanded that they should be given separate seat according to their number of population in local bodies, Provincial Legislative Council and Indian Legislative Assembly. Such move was also followed and supported by organizations formed among other tribes and backward communities like the Misings, Rabhas, Mataks and Morans, Chutiyas, Lalungs etc.

Assam Tribal League became a non-political organization by 1952, Henceforth; no central organization remained to fight for the common cause of tribal people. The impact of Assam Government aggressive move to make Assamese as compulsory state language was far-reaching. The leaders of Hills districts of undivided Assam formed 'All Party Hills Leaders Conference' (APHLC) and demanded a separate self-ruled state including all hills districts. Thus, Mizoram, Nagaland, and Meghalaya were separated from Assam at a different point in time. The authoritative administrative behaviour of high caste Hindu elite also created socio-cultural maladjustment among many other backward ethnic groups in Assam like the Morans, Mataks, Koch, Chutiya, Ahoms etc. and started their agitation and placed demand for special safeguard, treatment for themselves. Late Indira Gandhi's proposal to restructure Assam in the federal pattern was welcomed by tribal groups but immaterialized due to strong opposition from caste-Hindu Assamese elite group. Assam

Plains Tribal Council (PTCA) was formed in 1967 by demanding a separate autonomous state 'Udayachal' for plains tribes. PTCA showed its extreme view that without full political power for self-determination, development of tribal people is an impossible issue to resolve. Though PTCA represented all plains tribal people and also included the tea-tribal communities, in the practical field the Bodos and to some extent the Misings participated in the movement. But entering into parliamentary politics the magnitude of the PTCA movement reduced to nil gradually. Resented to such downturn of tribal leaders, United Tribal National Liberation Front (UTNLF) was formed in 1985 and All Bodo Student Union (ABSU) was formed in 1987 with the famous slogan 'divide Assam fifty-fifty'. While UTLNF remained dormant, ABSU earned extreme popularity in the course of time and the leadership transferred to students and lower stratum of Bodo society. Simultaneously, an extreme group of Bodo youth formed the militant group, Bodoland Security Force (BdSF, later renamed as NDFB) to fight for a separate country, the Bodoland. ABSU could draw the state and central government to its own favour and Bodoland Autonomous Council Act was signed for Bodo autonomy. But this treaty proved to be a fruitless and Bodo Liberation Tigers Force (BLTF), a militant group came into existence to fight for Bodo cause. BLTF came to an agreement with Government of Assam and formed Bodoland Territorial Council. Now, the Bodos are hoping for the best under the autonomy arrangement provided for them.

Towards the last decade of last century the tribal groups of the plains of Assam involved in a series of social movements for autonomous status in terms of development administration. Perceiving the anomaly in the distribution of development grants and benefits in the state plans the tribal groups demanded an arrangement of self-governance in terms of allocation of funds, access to revenue generation and access to some local resources, planning and implementation of development policies for themselves. One could see a series of activities like revival and enhancement of culture and tradition along with religious norms and language etc of these tribal groups leading towards a greater solidarity formation and sense of oneness. Such revivalism was accompanied with the creation of awareness regarding political rights and privileges offered by the Constitution of India to the tribal groups of the country and also towards the development denials relative to other non-tribal populations in the state. As result, a new form of autonomy outside the provision of 6th schedule of Indian constitution was awarded to the tribal groups of plains of Assam by the state government. Tribal groups including Mishing, Rabha, Tiwa, Thengal, Deori, Sonowal Kacharis availed the opportunity to implement their own development plans with central and state grants.

But the formation of such autonomous councils was not devoid of vested political interests of the ruling government and political parties. Unprecedented disturbance and conflicts have been continuing in the process of formation and running of these councils. The causes of masses have been set aside while fulfilling the interest of the tribal leaders and office bearers of the councils. The limited grants awarded by the government to different tribal councils have been mismanaged and misappropriated and tribal development, for which the councils were formed, has taken a back seat. In one sense the struggle for the real development of tribal people is not yet over. Rather it has taken a new shape and the conflict is now within and without.

Conclusion

The delineation of movement mentioned in the foregoing part shows some significant characteristics. In the first instance, the Moamoria revolt was an objectively derived movement cutting across the ethnic entities. This was a movement against the oppressor of a certain kind. Though it was a mass movement where peasants were the subjects, it was hardly against the class system itself. It was so because the leaders of the movement were feudal lord of a certain kind. Moreover, it was not against the system because, when the people could defeat the Royal force, they crowned a person called Ramakanta as their new king without making any desired or drastic change in the socio-political system of the kingdom. Most probably, their aim and ideology merged together and wanted a non-torturous king under the same arrangement. The movement did not produce a lasting result for some reasons, for example:

(i) There was no inherent ideology regarding political society to be established after the success of the movement.

(ii) The agent to be changed (here the royal domain) was not at all open to change and its quick retaliation and suppression could successfully destroy the movement.

(iii) The leadership, the Moamoria Mahantas, were quite reluctant to lead the movement and their ideology did not match the common people participated in the movement.

Acknowledging the limitation of the interpretation of the chapter the author would like to express the concern regarding the fabrication of history that limits the access to results and extent of events. New research with theoretical underpinning is need of the hour to document the real picture of such movements.

Likewise, the incidence of Patharughat was also an objective movement cutting across the subjective entities like caste and ethnic identities etc. It was objective because people were mobilized against land revenue and land alienation and land settlement. The subjects of the movement were categorically different from their leaders who were basically absentee landowners and landlords. Thus, instead of the similar interest of the two groups, the likely impact of the result of the movement was different. As there emerged law and order situation, the oppression was too harsh, As usual, the administration was not at all open for change. Thus, lack of leadership and lack of sustained ideology compounded with quick and stern reaction from the part of the government reduced the movement to naught.

Contrary to these two movements, the tribal assertion in Assam has been seen both as subjective as well as objective in its nature or typology. It is subjective in that such movements are based on ethnic identity, traditional culture, and customs. These are also objective in that the ultimate goal of such movements is related to economic development. We can see a host of a combination of theoretical underpinning in these movements. The revival of traditional socio-cultural components and looking for a newly formed political and social identity is very much fit into the Revitalization theory. Again, people's perception of negligence and lower social status attributed by non-tribal domain depicts the structural maladjustment of social domain causing a strain in socio-political structure of the society they live in. Above all, relative deprivation has been well conceived by these groups of people over a period of time making entire situation a product of the cyclic process. We can also fit this situation in 'injustice frame' propounded by culture theorists because there is a general trend accepted almost universally some sort of injustice has been done to the tribal and backward population across the world over a period of time by some social actor for which the tribal and backward communities are bound to assert for their social and political space in the contemporary world.

Amidst the superflow of modern theories of social movement, we can still find the relevance of old theories of social movement especially in developing and third world countries where poverty and income still remains a major factor in peoples' lives.

In the same tune, it is also very much true that market has been able to mould the socio-political life of people even in poorer and non-industrialized societies and countries across the world. Behind all socio-cultural struggles, demands, and aspirations one can see the market-oriented aspirations of such communities. Orientation or aspiration towards better education, service and employability, income generation, command over resources, health and well-being and infrastructure development which are very much present in the goals of most social movements are basically derivatives of domains controlled or at least influenced by the contemporary market system. All social responsibilities adhered to a welfare government are fulfilled basically exchanging the cost of such measures with marketable commodities and opening the socioeconomic domain for the expanding market domain in one or the other form. The widely talked about and widely used subjective entities like ethnic identities, tribal and caste solidarity etc are now nothing but some means of gaining a bargaining power to cope with situation created by growing market and trends of surrendering the public domain into the hand private domain controlled by market forces which even influence and directs big democracies like India.

Considering all these issues the task ahead for us is to analyze social movements considering all these components and set the trends of social movements in a more holistic way.

Notes

1. Moamoria or Mayamara is a religious school, an offshoot of Nava-Vaishnava religion propounded by Sri Sankardeva in Assam during 15th century AD. The influence of Moamoria religion has been very dominant in upper Assam, especially among the indigenous communities of Assam. It was propounded by Sri Aniruddha Deva.
2. *Satras* are the religious organizations established by the Nava-Vaishnava religious preachers in Assam. The head of the Satra is called Satradhikar, Gosai, Mahanta etc.
3. Ahoms were the Shan Tribe who entered present-day Assam in the early part of 12th century AD and ruled major parts of present-day Assam for nearly six hundred years. Their rule ended in 1826 when British East India Company took over the land from the Burmese King Ava who was defeated by the British army.
4. Common people (tenants) who pay land revenue

5. Village monastery established under the Nava-Vaishnava religious system where people assemble and recite the religious texts like the Kirtana, Bhagawata etc.
6. A way of salvation to God where the slaughter of animals, offering blood etc was quite common and it was believed that by satisfying gods and goddess by such sacrifices one can achieve energy and vigour.
7. A person who practices the art of satisfying deities with hymns and magic etc.
8. A business community hailing from Marwar of Rajasthan.
9. The biggest and longest river flows through east to west of Assam.
10. Assembly of people.
11. Administrative units to collect land revenue of certain demarcated areas. The officer is called *Mauzadar*.

References

Aberle, David F. 1966, *The Peyote Religion among the Navaho*. Chicago: Aldine.

Baden-Powel, BH. 1895. *The Land System of British India*. Vol III, London.

Blumer, Herbert G. 1969. 'Collective behavior'. In Alfred McClung Lee, (Ed): *Principles of Sociology*. pp. 65-121, Third Edition. New York: Barnes and Noble Books.

Habermas, J. 1981. 'New social movements', *Telos*. 40:33-37.

Heberle, Rudolph, 1951. *Social Movement: An Introduction to Political Sociology*. New York: Appleton-Century-Crafts.

Lewis, Kilhan, 1964, 'Social Movements'. In Robert Faris (Ed): *Handbook of Modern Sociology*. Chicago.

Mauss, Armand, L. 1975. *Social Problems and Social Movements*. Philadelphia: Lippincott.

Rao, MS. 2008, 'Conceptual problems in the study of social movements'.In MS Rao (Ed): *Social Movements in India*. pp 1 – 6, Delhi, Manohar.

Ryan, Charlotte and William W Gamson, 2006 'The art of reframing political debates'. *Contexts*, 5 (1): 13-18.

Smelser, N. 1962. *Theory of Collective Behaviour*. London: Routledge and Kegan Paul.

Tilly, Charles, 1978. *From Mobilization to Revolution*. Reading. Massachusetts: Addison-Wesley.

Touraine, Alain, 1995, 'Democracy: From a politics to citizenship to a politics of recognition', In Louis Maheu (Ed): *Social Movements and Social Classes: The Future of Collective Action*, SAGE Studies in International Sociology. London: Sage Publication.

Wallace, Anthony. 1956. 'Revitalization movements'. *American Anthropologist* 58: 264-281.

CHAPTER - 2

INTROSPECTING THE SOCIAL IDENTITY MOVEMENT

CHANDANA BHATTACHARJEE AND SURAJIT SEN

The German Sociologist Lorenz von Stein introduced the term 'social movements' in 1850 in his book '*History of the French Social Movement from 1789 to the Present*'. Social movements are meant simply to bring a better life for the members of the society. American Civil Rights Movement is one of the most famous social movements of the 20th Century, from the point of view of history. Our presentation intends to relook at or puts forth a changed perspective on social movements – originating from identity consciousness, assertion ranging from ethnic identity to religious identity and beyond. Social movements are at times essential to ascertain the existence and sustainability of any society, but it is also essential today to pause a while and make an honest, unbiased attempt to assess the justification and achievements of those in our country since independence. Albeit, it is not possible to narrate here every social movement since independence, yet the ever-increasing tendency of conflict among the people tells the tale of general unhappiness that persists. The conflicts are manifested at different levels. Our viewpoints, unlike most of the empirical data-based narration on social movements, takes into consideration the emerging trends and fast developing situations which raise the very basic question regarding identity, and as such, the identity movements.

'Identity' is a generic term used in Social Sciences. This umbrella term can be broadly related to:

1. A person's self-image, self-esteem, individuality; and
2. the concept of role behaviour

The former is commonly used for psychoanalysis asserting on 'personal identity', i.e. the characteristic composition that makes a person unique. 'Social identity' on the other hand is an instrument of the sociologists to describe the functional work of roles of an individual in the social milieu. Whatever be the discipline-specific approach, a secular approach has to be adopted to deal with the issue of identity both at the level of individual cognition and of collective behaviour. The term 'identity' became of much interest to the anthropologists with the emergence of modern concerns with ethnicity and social movements during the 1970s.

It is evident from the uses of the term 'identity' that we cannot do away with the concept of 'identity', rather use it scientifically and rationally. 'Identity' is an abstract concept; it is also flexible and volatile.

An 'ethnic group' in very simple language means those who belong to or follow a distinctive cultural tradition. Following this definition, 'tribals' do also form such ethnic groups. However, the phrase 'who are tribals', becomes a pertinent question. It is not to be misinterpreted as though we denying the existence of tribe as a social unit. Generalizing the various definitions, we understand that they are:

1. Economically self-sufficient
2. Use primitive technology
3. Geographically isolated
4. Have a common dialect/language
5. Have a traditional political and judicial system

Tribal solidarity is a point of strength for these groups of people. 'Scheduled Tribes' are those who are enlisted in the Vth and VIth schedules of India's Constitution. The schedules secure these groups of people with certain provisions. Some of these provisions for these ethnic groups were taken from the 1874 Act (Scheduled Districts), Government of India Acts 1919 and 1935. These were the systematic strategies adopted by the British administrators during the colonial rule intending to pacify the upsurge of Paharias of Rajmahal Hills (1872), Ho Mutiny of Singhbum (1831), Khond Uprising (1846) and the famous Santhal Uprising (1855) in Central India, to name a few. The British Indian Government was also forced to send punitive expeditions during 1850-1890 to suppress the people of Assam, Nagaland and Jaintia Hills; again to the Lushai Hills and to the Abor during the last part of the 19th Century and first part of 20th Century. The British measures and policies were directed to suppress the resistance of these ethnic groups in the Northeastern part of India. These policies for these people were carried over to post independent plans of our country. Inspired by V. Elwin, the famous *Panchsheel* of the then Prime Minister Pandit Jawaharlal Nehru was a sketch on the same line. Piles of the document are available to justify the statement.

We divert, therefore, our attention from the documented 'goodies' and intend to record our observation in these regards. The Constitutional safeguards provided for the tribals under the various plans are undoubtedly praiseworthy attempt to bring the so-called 'tribal' set of the population – the otherwise known as economically, educationally, politically backward people at par with the advanced communities. The conflict is apparently inherent. On the one side, it is to maintain ingenuity of the tribal people, and on the other, to pull them up in every respect of life. The ingenuity of tribals or tribal identity versus advancement leaves a lot of scopes to be debated.

The key theme of the present treatise is 'Social Movements'. Going by the traditional ways of understanding, all kinds of movements originate from the challenged identity, which could be felt from any viewpoint. This varies from 'singular identity' to 'plural (identity) affiliation'. Plural affiliations are adjusted to adapt oneself to the complexity of the society. The traditional movements that are rooted in the economic deprivation (Karl Marx) alone have been faded rather than losing its relevance. The demands of the movements are now based on multiple reasons – more precisely bearing the nature of power-orientation in terms of political, economic, religious, etc. at the same time. However, grasp of economic and political power happens to be the primary goal.

Every social movement begins with pretty good intention – ideal leaders, genuine causes, admirable ideologies, ideal paths laid for work, etc. the movements grow old by age and many such ideal concepts are lost on its way. A number of social movements in India, to refer, along with so many movements in our country, particularly since independence, raise the moot question that 'does a successful movement bring satisfaction to all the members of the society?' or 'Do they feel they have achieved what they have fought for?' or even 'Could any such movement secure any ethnic identity?' Creating a *classless society* (Karl Marx) is a utopia. This sounds more like the concept of 'heaven' – the artistic culmination of all good, merely an imagination. All the social movements in our country since independence have created distinctly the two polar opposite classes in any society – the 'haves' and the 'have-nots' (Karl Marx). In between, of course, lays a number of other categories with their respective identities. There is no one instance where such movements have not created new identities and new challenges to their existence.

'Identity' itself is a flexible term – created, attached and detached according to one's conscience. The fact is that people identify with the group sharing certain interests; the same also does fall apart whenever their interest differs. And this could be the sole reason behind the death of many social movements, and also many movements reshape to the level of insurgency. This shift is very much observed in parts of Northeast India. *Bodos* have achieved partially, yet striving for more. *Naga* society is fragmented on this issue, Manipur has torn apart, and some other movements in the state of Assam depict the similar characteristics.

Identity, in the present day, is much more a complex question. Defining singular identity as well as collective identity desperately requires being re-looked at with the advent of globalization too.

Globalization has opened up new vistas altogether for the people irrespective of any identity concern – be it socioeconomic, religious, linguistic, territorial and so on and so forth. The concept of 'pure ethnic group' will soon become an illusion as is the concept of 'pure race'. New kind of education (profession-oriented education), alien medium of instruction (now our own tongue, modern gadgets and every new technology that we use today, the types of jobs to which people are employed, limitless migration to different parts of the world, inter-community marriage, all these and much more, have added to the confusion in understanding 'identity'. As an obvious result – identifying an ethnic group or even identifying an individual with his/her root (uprooted). The urban zone people follow mixed culture while the people in the periphery can rather identify themselves in a more organized manner. Ethnic identity-based social movements today, in fact, are more politically geared where mass involvement could be traced more as a whim, i.e. without making many attempts to rationalize the totality of the movement. The inevitable result is that the society is seen developing more and more internal conflicts adding to its disadvantages. Revivalist movements (e.g. Seng Khasi movement in Meghalaya) though do not exhibit such conflict within, yet the pace of movement did not gain momentum at any point of time and, therefore, its impact has been limited.

Movements, the nature of which may either be democratic or undemocratic, both, however, have a negative impact on the society wheresoever's it is organized. Undemocratic movements are more of violent nature, whereas democratic movements are supposed to be peaceful protests. Yet we observe in both the kinds of movement violence and destruction; only the difference of violence between the two is measured in degrees. Both these types hamper the socio-economic development of the concerned group of people. If reasonably analyzed, the entire canvas of the country, including Northeastern part of India for that matter, have done hardly any good to its people, rather have destroyed a number of families, public properties, government properties, killed people at random, taken away all peace of mind, left the people with nightmarish history and tales. The advantage seekers conveniently ignore to reckon their own peoples' miseries for it does not match their interests. The presence of classes in Northeast India is as much evident today as in any other parts of the country, the region comprised of a number of tribal communities, traditionally characterized as 'egalitarian'.

'Deprived' is a word that is inlaid in every mind of the inhabitants of the Northeastern region. Seclusion and reservation policies carried over from the colonial rule, enhancement of the provisions for the development of the tribals in the Constitution, more and more fund allocation for the states of this region by the centre for its development, five-year plans since independence, unrecognized, used and misused over the decades narrates a pathetic history of the Northeastern region of India. The grievances aggravated every time and the feeling of 'deprivation' works instantly without many realizations. 'Who deprives' is the prime question of which people have the knowledge and understanding through yet a conscious silence is maintained in this regard certainly fearing powerful people. Indeed, it has always been convenient to unite a group by pointing against 'other groups'. Unfortunately, traditional methods of wooing the people still are very functional. Measuring by that yardstick, we have stepped far beyond any limit of crises, many of which are caused from within.

Globalization has brought economic, political, educational, technological and other changes that have also taught many among us to think beyond the narrow boundaries of self-interests. A new trend of movements are now found in many societies which consider human societies – which consider human rights over selfish causes, which fight for animal rights, saving the environment, etc projecting much above than being a mere man. These kinds of movements have much wider causes, embraces much more areas for developing, restraining, creating awareness among the people in general. These kinds of movements are fast gaining momentum worldwide. These are the neo-social movements also seeking its ground even in Northeastern India which can be said to be a ray of hope.

Documents Consulted

Bhattacharjee, Chandana, 1996. *Ethnicity and Autonomy Movement – A Case of Bodo-Kacharis of Assam*, Vikas Publishing House Pvt. Ltd., New Delhi.

Polletta, F., and JM. Jasper, 2001, Collective Identity and Social Movements, *Annual Reviews Sociology*, University of North California, Vol. 27.

Sen, Amartya, 2006. *Identity and Violence: The Illusion of Destiny*, Penguin Group, London.

Sharma, BB., 2002. *Tribal Affairs in India: A Crucial Transition*, Sahyog Pustok Kutir (Trust), New Delhi.

Chapter - 3

Religious Reform Movements in Arunachal Pradesh: Understanding Adi and Mishmi Tribes

Tarun Mene and S.K. Chaudhuri

A movement or social movements are a type of group action with a common ideology who act together to achieve certain general goals relating to political issues, social issues, etc. It is generally designed to bring about or resist primary changes in an existing society or group. This may be of various types such as reform movement, radical movement, the environmental movement, tribal movement, caste movement, etc. Not intending to go deeper in defining the conceptual and typology of social movement as such which is beyond the frame of the present chapter, let it be clear at the very outset that the main discursive discourses will focus on the religious reform movements among the two selected ethnic tribal group of Arunachal Pradesh, such as, the Adis and the Idu Mishmis. It will precisely deal with the situation which arises as a result of a confrontation between traditional system of thought and practices and the values and the contradictory modern elements that have penetrated into the tribal world. And finally, try to generalize the results of such religious reform movement which are accelerated to redress the existing changes in the society and in this process of reform how the concerned ethnic group emulates certain elements of greater religion into their own fold thereby giving rise to the institutionalization of tribal religion.

Reform movements in the context of the tribe have a long history in India and Northeast India in particular. In his two edited volumes, Singh (1982) has provided us with various tribal movements in India that took place at different time intervals. In the first volume which entirely deals with tribal movements in Northeast India, not a single paper we find that talks about the situation in Arunachal Pradesh, except Sarkar (1982) who dealt with the rise of identity consciousness among few selected tribes of the state. However, the author presented the overall discussion in a journalistic frame[1]. For such absence of writing in the context of Arunachal Pradesh, it may be assumed that whatsoever movements we observe today is of very recent origin. However, it is worth mentioning, as Sarkar (1982) presented in his writing that how identity consciousness among the tribes of Arunachal Pradesh gained its momentum at the very early time (date back to 1950s) but attained as a movement in very recent time. In the context of Arunachal Pradesh, we do not find any major movement except the movements of formalization/institutionalization of tribal religion and script movement at various occasions in recent time and the present chapter basically deals with the first one.

The Genesis of Religious Reform Movement in Arunachal Pradesh

The religious reform movements in Arunachal Pradesh may be marked with the beginning of the centralized or community-based celebration of festivals by the various tribal ethnic groups. It may be said that the need for such overall structural change in the celebration of the festival could be understood in terms of identity issue but it is as well as a response to the confrontation between traditional system of thought and practices and the values and demands of a modernizing state, society, and culture. Festivals like Solung of Adis, Reh, and Kemeha of Idu Mishmi, Dree of Apatani,

Nyokum of Nyishi, etc, in its traditional form, were basically family, clan or village-based festivals but its up gradation to community level is essential for the preservation of both sacred and secular dimensions of festival and its multiple folk genres, viz. dances, songs, chanting, myth, ritual offerings etc. As festival symbolizes collective performances, often centering around certain ritual operations, it cannot be identified as a separate unit from the institution of religion in a broader perspective. Hence, it is in this sense that the rising self-consciousness of tribal people towards festivals may be looked at as the marker of religious reform movements in the context of Arunachal Pradesh. If we look back into the past, such trend of concretization of festivals dates as far back to 1958 where an effort was made to bring the Adi festival called Solung to the community level[2]. Similarly, festivals like Nyokum Yullow of the Nyishi, Reh festival of the Idu Mishmi, and Si-Donyi of Tagin tribe were brought to community level during 1967, 1968 and 1975 respectively.[3] This is as well as a movement; a movement of tribal ethnic groups which cannot be looked at simply in terms of the development of identity consciousness alone but rather need to be understood as a movement of revivalism and reformism of the traditional institutions of the local people.

Secondly, with the advent of various elements of outside world such as post-colonial administration, the process of modernization, education and particularly the process of conversion to other religion, the traditional religious institution of most of the tribal community of Arunachal Pradesh underwent a spectacular change. The coming up of an institutionalized form of greater religion such as Christianity, Hinduism at the local level have not only influenced few sections of people to convert but also initiated the process of reformation in the traditional belief and practices in the form of religious institutionalization movement. As a result, the emerging movements for the institutionalization of indigenous belief and practices of the various tribal community such as *Donyipoloism* among the Tani tribe such as Adi, Nyishi, Galo, Apatani etc, *Intayaism* among the Idu Mishmis, *Rangfraim* among Tangsa tribe, gained momentum as religious reform movement of old traditional beliefs and practices. In this regard, Blackburn (2002) rightly pointed out that 'Perhaps the most fundamental change is that animistic beliefs and rituals are undergoing formalization into a 'religion' with new visual images, places of worship, and a formal theology. This systematization of the worship of Donyi-Polo (Sun-Moon) places it alongside the other religions known in the area: Christianity, Buddhism, and Hinduism. Ritual practitioners have also formed a state-wide association of shamans. These changes are fast-paced and largely undocumented.'[4] Such movements in Arunachal Pradesh are not only true in the sphere of religion but also observed in other aspects. For example, the change in nomenclature of many tribes in Arunachal Pradesh such as Abor to Adi, Dafla to Nyishi, Gallong to Galo, etc suggests that people are now in search of social identity adding a new social formation of ethnic groups in the contemporary situation. Earlier, various scholars like Bhagabati (1990: 224) noted that identity consolidation involving a number of distinct tribes is found in Arunachal Pradesh taking the example of Gallong, the Padam, the Minyong, the Pasi, etc called themselves as Adi (literally 'hills men'). But such consolidation is weakening in modern days due to various socio-political reasons. So-called Gallong known earlier as a sub-tribe of larger consolidated Adi tribe now prefers to recognize themselves as Galo with an independent identity as a tribe with the help of constitutional amendment.

With the formation of various state-wide NGOs, Associations, Society, etc, one may confirm the ongoing process of religious reform movements in Arunachal Pradesh. The formation of All Arunachal Pradesh Abotani Nibu (priest) Welfare Association, Donyi-Polo Yelam Kebang, Donyi Polo Welfare Association, Donyi Polo Mission, etc and community-based societies like Idu Mishmi Cultural and Literary Society (IMCLS), Adi Cultural and Literary Society (ACLS), etc no doubt accelerated the various social-political movement of the concerned ethnic group of the State. Most of such associations have concentrated on the issues of indigenous religion and its specialists such as shamans. It not only suggests the concern and pursuit of the ethnic group of the frontier state regarding identity issue and preservation of tradition and culture but also reflects how people are involving themselves in the visible process of religious reform movement in the state with rising societal consciousness with collective effort and as well shift in attitude towards agents of change.

The infliction of ideas and philosophies of greater religion on the little tradition is well reflected in many writings as well. It is interesting to note how Hindu legends are linked up with the Idu Mishmi culture. Singh (1995:16) highlighting the Rukmini legend informs, 'The Idu Mishmis bear the mark of punishment inflicted on them by Krishna himself because they had opposed his marriage with Rukmini. The story suggests that the Idu Mishmis followed the Bhishmak tradition through centuries'. Similarly, Behera (2008/1994, pp 190-191) informs that 'the Idus - a subgroup of the Mishmi tribe has developed a distinct ethnic identity around the legend of Rukmini and gradually they were made to believe themselves Yaduvanshi'. Here Rukmini is said to descend/ progeny of the Idus to whom Lord Krishna married. However, no one finds mention of Rukmini or Krishna in any form which is embedded in Idu culture. If there had been any such relationship between the Idus and Lord Krishna or with the Bhishmak traditional then there should have been some ritualistic attribution, folklore or folktale, myth, etc, may be in the chanting of shaman relating such linkages. But such elements are completely absent in the Idu Mishmi culture. This is precisely the way through which Hinduised ideas are inflicted on the Idu Mishmis by the Hindu missionaries as it is evident through the invented images of Inni, the sun goddess of Idu Mishmi. Such information also has its impact on many Idu intellectual, young scholars who are not only trying to rectify such misleading information but also engaged themselves in the process of reform movements.

Religious Reform Movement among the Idu Mishmi and Adi Tribe

No doubt that any movement always gets started when the established social norms and systems and values of the social group are harmed or disturbed that led to change by the various agents which may be internally or externally executed. To Idu Mishmi society till now it is mostly the external factors that compelled people to organize themselves into groups, associations, etc and initiated them to lead movements against the agents of change in the society. Of course, with the advent of socio-economic and political development processes in the Idu Mishmi inhabiting region, appreciated and welcomed changes are observable in various sociocultural aspects, however, we find the serious defiant move from within the society when changes are gradually brought in the sphere of religion. The process of conversion to Christianity remained one of the most important factors which helped in giving birth to religious reform movement among the Idu Mishmi tribe. There are many instances where people demolished Churches, protested against the construction of a church in the villages, destruction of musical instruments like guitar, physical assaults and threatening to Christian Brothers and Father etc[5]. With all such happenings, the realization came to people for serious effort concerning surviving and functionality of Idu religion and as such concretization of Idu Mishmi religion in a systematic manner was initiated which gave birth to religious reform movement among the Idu Mishmi tribe.

This movement may be termed as *Nani Innitayaism*[6] among the Idu Mishmi[7] tribe where an effort has been made to create images of *Innitaya* or *Maselo Zenu* (the sun) whom Idu consider as a supreme goddess. It is to mention here that the underpinned idea for the systematic and formalization of traditional religion was first propounded during 1968 by late

Ita Pulu, a renowned social activist of Idu community but without much practicality. The organized rhythm of the movement got serious and real momentum in the Idu inhabiting region only around the middle of 1990s onwards by various organizations such as Idu Cultural and Literary Society (ICLS), Vikas Parishad members, All Idu Mishmi Students Union (AIMSU), public leaders, local people of various status, etc[8]. This movement gave birth to an image of Supreme Goddess *Inni,* which embodies the highest ethical conception reach by the Idus with the conceptualization of new terminology of *Nani Innitaya* which is used to represent the Idu religion. It started with a similar pattern of Hindu form of religious attributions such as propitiating invented image of Inni Goddess, prayers, use of incense sticks, adoration of image with flowers, the lighting of candles and *diyas* (earthen lamp), etc. Today one may find an image of *Nani Innitaya* hung in many Idu houses which of course suggest that the movement had its impact, though not at large. A serious effort is not reflective in *Innitayaism* movement of the Idu Mishmis in comparison to the ongoing movement of *Donyipoloism* that is taking place among the Tani group of tribes such as Adi, Apatani, Nyishi, etc. However quest for the institutionalization of Idu religion is a serious concern for the people and such movement is obscurely still active and is in the everyday discussion of the Idu individuals, among groups, NGOs, Associations etc. At various occasions, community-based Idu Cultural and Literary Society (ICLS) have organized seminars, meetings, etc concerning various issues such as preservation, promotion, and upliftment of tradition and culture, protection of the institution of the shaman, preservation of local dialect and promotion of its invented Roman script, etc.

Similar to the Idu Mishmis, most of the causes of the religious reform movement among the Adi tribe may be attributed to the external agents such as socio-economic and political development processes and most importantly the advent of greater religion specially Christianity which have, one way or otherwise, entered the traditional tribal world and started to split the social relations which is regarded as the base of the tribal society. Unlike the Idu Mishmis, the introduction of Christianity in the Adi belt dates back to early part of 20th century and the Padams a subgroup of Adi tribe was the first to embrace it inhabiting the plains of Lower Dibang Valley District of Arunachal Pradesh. With the passage of time, it started spreading to another part of Adi region and its impact was so afflictive for some section of Adi tribe that it sparked many instances of social unrest on many occasions. We find as many as twenty-one cases of destruction, dismantlement, banning and burning down of churches and other cases such as imposition of fine up to Rs 200 for those who adopts Christian religion, extortion/cessation of property, Judiciary cases among the Christian and non-Christian were reported in various Adi inhabiting areas in between 1969 to 1985[9]. Such incidence clearly reflects the deep intensity of protective movements initiated by the locals themselves which afterward gave rise to the religious reform movement in the Adi inhabiting region.

The ongoing movement called *Donyipoloism* among the Adi tribe[10], under the umbrella of *Donyi-Polo Yelam Kebang* (a voluntary organization of the Adi community established on 31st December 1986 at Pasigaht[11]) started propagating *Donyi- Polo* (Sun and Moon) cult in an organized manner at *Gangging* (like temple for Hinduism) considering it as a central place for worship with written texts with numbers of sacred songs (Rukbo, 1999). They have maintained a regular prayer day on Saturday every week and textualized their oral tradition in the form of a book called *Angun Bedang* which is perceived to be sacred similar to Bible, Koran, Gita of greater religion for the popularization of such belief systems. Taabe Abu, the priest who is basically the community shaman led the gathering at *Gangging*. The basic materials required during prayer time or at the *Gangging* include *Asi* (water), *Ambin* (rice), *Riidin* (a variety of creeper), *Toti Bangko* (a sacred plant), *Emul* (a metallic star-shaped object worn in the neck), candles, incense sticks, etc. They have formalized some basic moral code of conduct which needs to be followed at *Gangging*. In almost all traditional religious activities such as rituals related to healing, marriage, childbirth, death construction of house they have adopted some slight modifications. Almost in all the villages in Siang belt, this formalized practice of *Donyipoloism* is observable. Incorporation of such ideas is primarily aimed to protect and preserve the traditional belief and practices. However, the main emphasis adopted by this Donyi-Polo movement is to establish a direct relationship between man and Supreme Being called Donyi-Polo, the Sun, and Moon God, with the help of priest called Taabe Abu abandoning the traditional belief in evil spirits and ritual practice of offerings and animal sacrifice to them. Such initiative is basically in response to encountering the process of conversion activities of tribal people by the missionaries and other similar agencies. These shielding efforts of the locals to preserve traditional belief system have again brought up a new philosophical contradiction within the followers of *Donyipoloism.* While working on the Adi Tangams of Tuting, Jedo and Kugging village of Upper Siang District, the researcher had found that the inflow of the institutionalized form of *Donyipoloism* and even Christianity had already entered maximum families in the villages but on the contrary still there are families who claimed that they are neither follower of Donyi-Polo nor Christianity. However, for this section of people, the ultimate supreme creator or God remained Donyi and Polo (Sun and Moon) but interestingly they detached themselves from an institutionalized form of *Donyipoloism* in terms of professing and systematization of propitiation. Such attitude of people simply reflects the ideological contradictions within the followers of Donyi-Polo religion itself. Such ideological polarity is clearly visible even between the Christian and non-Christian followers of different affiliation in any given tribal community.

Conclusions

This discourse on the religious reform movement is in fact, part of the ongoing change which is taking place among the tribes of Arunachal Pradesh. So far, the distinct reform in the religious terrain is concerned, undoubtedly, Adis are the pioneer which was led by the late Talom Rukbo, who initiated the Donyi-Polo movement with the formation of *Ganggings* which can be located in different villages of the Adi inhabited areas. This has influenced the Mishmis, and many other tribes, like, Nyishis, Tangsas, Galos, who also invented images[12] and created the textual basis of indigenous belief and practices which were part of indigenous traditional religion.

Notes

1. Sarkar JN (1982) '*Development of Identity Consciousness in Arunachal Pradesh*', in KS. Singh (1982).
2. Sarkar, 1982; p233. Though Sarkar did not refer to Solung festival as such the Adi Tribe celebrate Solung festival according to Christian calendar on Sep 1st every year.
3. Referred to Unpublished M.A (Anthropology) and M.Phil dissertations at Arunachal Institute of Tribal Studies, Rajiv Gandhi University by Ashan Riddi on *Indigenous Institutions of the Tagins,* Nime Taba on *Nyokum at Sagalee; A Study on the Festival of the Nyishis* and Tarun Mene on *Reh Festival of the Idu Mishmis.*
4. Stuart Blackburn, II AS News Letter | #29 | November 2002.
5. It was during 2000 at Anini some group of local youth destructed one Baptist Chruch. During 1997 one Leeta Linggi, aged around 60, male, of Iduli village died after prolong illness. As his wife was converted to Baptist Christian, she decided to perform the funeral of her husband in the Christian system. To this decision, a serious disagreement and conflicting situation arose among the kin relatives of deceased and his wife and villagers as well. This incident became a history in the Idu community for it was the first Christian funeral given to an Idu Mishmi individual. The Christian Father and others who were there for the funeral performances were threatened and their musical instruments were also destroyed by the people. However, at last, the deceased

was buried in Christian system and later on a ritual called *Bro-Fri* was performed in traditional Idu religion.

6. The concept of Nani Innitaya is coined from the term *Innitaya* or *Maselo Zenu* (the sun) to whom the Idus regard as a supreme goddess. The prefix *Nani* meaning Mother is added to it to create a sense of supreme authority as to the concept of *Ma Durga, Ma Kali* in Hinduism where *Ma* meaning Mother.
7. Both the terminology 'Idu' and 'Mishmi' have no concrete and specific meaning in Idu language. Baruah (1960, p 98) mentioned that 'the word Idu, is most probably a distortion of the word Midu which means inhabitant of Idu Valley and is the name for only one section of the people'. It is here to mention that Idus may be categorized into three groups as per their dialectic variation and in few words meaning which` are *Mindri, Mithu,* and *Midu*. Most of the *Mindri* speaking Idus inhabits the present Upper Dibang Valley District around Dri and Mathu river valley. The *Mithu* inhabits on both sides of the Ithun river valley. The *Midu* speaking Idus are mainly found in lower foothills and lower valleys of Mishmi Hills. So most probably, *Midu* speaking Idus of lower foothills and valleys first came in contact with outsiders and only from their dialectic nomenclature *'Midu'* the term 'Idu' was coined to designate the tribe. As I put it *Mithu* speaking Idus inhabits Ithun Valley, Baruah (*ibid*, p 11) designated the same Idus of Ithun Valley as *Bebejiyas*, again the term which has no concrete meaning and origin in Idu language. And for the term 'Mishmi', Bhattacharjee (1983, p 13) suggested that there is no clarity of origin of the term though largely believed that it has been coined by the people of plains of Assam to designate the tribe. Further, one may find that Idus refer to themselves as *Kera-A*. Here *Kera* is believed to be a name of ancestral forefather and *A* stands for children and thereby meaning children of Kera.
8. In one occasion somewhere in 1997-98 the researcher himself witnessed the inaugural programme where some eminent figure of the Idu society offered Hindu form/pattern of puja to the created image of *Nani Innitaya* in Rekho, the community hall at Cheta Village, Roing, the District Headquarters of Lower Dibang Valley District.
9. Pertin (2006) pp, 19-21.
10. Adi (Hills men) tribe was formerly known as Abor (unruly and savage) which is no more in use. As a consolidated tribe, it has numbers of subgroup like Padam, Minyong, Pasi, Karko, Simong, Millang, Bori-Bokar, Komkar, Tangam, etc. They are mainly concentrated in East Siang, West Siang, Upper Siang, in the foothills of Lower Dibang Valley Districts of Arunachal Pradesh.

11. Rukbo (1999) pp. 35.
12. For detail one can look at the paper presented by Chaudhuri (2009) in a national conference on the Spirit of Northeast India organized by the IGNCA, New Delhi in January 2009.

References

Baruah, TK. 1960. *The Idu Mishmis*, Directorate of Research, Government of Arunachal Pradesh, Itanagar.

Behera MC and SK Chaudhuri. 1998. *Indigenous Faiths and Practices of the Tribes of Arunachal Pradesh*, Himalayan Publication, Itanagar.

Behera, MC 2008. 'Diverse cultural adaptations in the tribal societies of Arunachal Pradesh', *Journal of Social Anthropology*, 5: 189-198.

Bhagabati, AC .1990, 'Tribal transformation in Assam and Northeast India: An appraisal of emerging ideological dimensions'. In B. Chaudhuri (Ed): *Tribal Transformation in India; Ethnopolitical and Identity Crisis,* pp 487-509, Vol-III, Inter-India Publication, New Delhi.

Bhagabati, AC.1990. 'Emergent tribal identity in Northeast India'. In Buddhadeb Chaudhuri (Ed): *Tribal Development in India*, pp 213-232, Inter India Publications, New Delhi.

Blackburn, S, II AS News Letter | #29 | November 2002

Borang, K. 2004. 'Philosophy of Donyi Polo', In T. Mibang and SK Chaudhuri (Eds): *Understanding of Tribal Religion*. Mittal Publications, New Delhi.

Chaudhuri, SK. 2008. 'Plight of the Igus: Notes on shamanism among the Idu Mishmi tribe of Arunachal Pradesh, India', *European Bulletin of Himalayan Research,* 32: 84-108.

Chaudhury, S., and DK. Duarah. 2004. 'Religious beliefs and institution of priesthood among the tribes of Arunachal Pradesh'. In T.Mibang and SK. Chaudhuri (Ed): *Understanding Tribal Religion,* pp 19-34, Mittal Publications, New Delhi.

Chaudhuri, SK.2009a. 'From Igu to Intaya', In S. Dutta and B.Tripathy (Eds): *Religious History of Arunachal Pradesh,* Gyan Publishing House, New Delhi.

Chaudhuri, SK. 2009b. *Inventing Images and Reforming Tribal Religion*, unpublished paper.

Das NK, 2003, *Culture, Religion, and Philosophy: Critical Studies in Syncretism and Inter-Faith Harmony*, Rawat Publication, New Delhi.

Durkheim, E. 1971. *The Elementary Forms of the Religious Life,* George Allen and Unwin Ltd, London.

Ering, O .2004. 'Philosophy of Donyi Polo', In T. Mibang and S.K. Chaudhuri (Eds): *Understanding of Tribal Religion,* Mittal Publication, New Delhi.

Natarajan, Nalini.1982, 'Culture revivalism among the Christian Khasis of Meghalaya'. In KS. Singh (Ed): *Tribal Movements in India,* Vol-I, pp 151-172, Manohar Publication, New Delhi.

Pertin Ojing. 2006. *Impact of Christianity in Adi Society (A case study of Mirbuk Village, East Siang District, Pasighat, Arunachal Pradesh),* Unpublished M.A Dissertation, Arunachal Institute of Tribal Studies, Rajiv Gandhi University.

Rukbo Talom. 1999. 'Institutionalization of a Tradition: Donyi-poloyelam Kebang: A Case Study'. In *Traditional Systems of Northeast India* (Dec 1999, pp 33-39), Seminar Booklet on Traditional Systems: Change and Continuity held at Along, West Siang District, Arunachal Pradesh organized by Vivekananda Kendra Institute of Culture, Guwahati.

Sarkar, JK. 1982, 'Development of identity consciousness in Arunachal Pradesh', In KS. Singh (Ed): *Tribal Movements in India,* Vol-I, pp 231-239. Manohar Publication, New Delhi.

Singh, KS.1982. *Tribal Movements in India,* Vol I and II. Manohar Publication, New Delhi.

Singh, KS. 1995. *People of India, Arunachal Pradesh,* Volume - XIV, Anthropological Survey of India, Calcutta.

Traditional Systems of Northeast India. December 1999, Seminar Booklet on Traditional Systems: Change and Continuity held at Along, West Siang District, Arunachal Pradesh organized by Vivekananda Kendra Institute of Culture, Guwahati.

Chapter - 4

Industrial Labour Movements: A Study of the Tea Garden Labourers of the Brahmaputra Valley, Assam

Rudraman Thapa

As a part of the social movements, the industrial labour class movements have gained substantial momentum in the contemporary electoral politics of the State more specifically in the post-colonial era. Fragmented into two transparent segments viz. the organized and unorganized sectors, the industrial labour class of people is commonly branded as the blue-collar and white-collar workers in both the sectors. While the former comprises the labourers connected with the physical work, the latter entangled with the office work instead of manual labour in industries[1]. Nonetheless, so far as the industrial labour class in organized sector is concerned, they have been building up a variety of movements as the effective means of redressing their manifold grievances and pent-up frustrations. And while undertaking such ventures the industrial labour class usually appeared to have come under the straight influence of political parties especially in the event of getting themselves consolidated, organized as well as disciplined under an innovative banner what is popularly designated as the trade unions. As such, the industrial labour class movements in India, particularly in the post-colonial era, came to be known as the trade union movements. These movements were exclusively dominated and steered by the enlightened leaders associated with the various political parties but interestingly who themselves did not belong to the labour class[2]. In this way, as soon as the industrial labour class movements in India came under the grip of the politically ambitious leaders, the movements invariably had become politicized. Virtually speaking, building up an industrial labour class movement in the state can be termed as a potential forum for the realization of well-orchestrated political agenda of the concerned political parties. Keeping this development in mind, the present article is intended to examine the social movements built up by the tea industrial labour class in Assam under the stewardship of the *Assam Chah Mazdoor Sangha* the leading tea trade union of the Congress (I) that represents the Tea Garden Labourers of the Brahmaputra Valley of the State.

II

Initiation of tea plantation in 1837 in upper Assam by the British colonial masters and their eventual departure left behind an enduring legacy of the same in the State. As is well known that a huge number of the impoverished tribal people imported from other parts of India, and employed them as the indentured labourers in Assam tea plantation remained illiterate and disorganized for a long time. Virtually speaking, the Tea Garden Labourers (hereinafter to be referred as the TGLs) were strategically and premeditatedly kept squarely lagging behind so as to facilitate the continuation of long-term objective of tea plantation and thereby perpetuating the colonial mastery over the TGLs. Such well-calculated strategy eventually made the British tea planters successful in their mission. This pathetic plight of the TGLs, nonetheless, did not remain irreversible since the decolonization of the country followed by the universalization of education and democratization of politics that obviously paved the way for the growth of awareness among the TGLs[3]. Of course, it is interesting to note that initiative in this direction was undertaken by the various political parties under the banner of their respective trade unions. For instance, the Indian National Trade Union Congress (INTUC) was founded on 4 May 1947 affiliated to the Indian National Congress (INC) party with the sole object of looking after the industrial labour class welfare. It's Assam branch was floated on 3 September of the same year with Kamalapati Tripathy as its founder chairperson. Likewise, other political parties were also not lagging behind in opening trade unions with the pretext of looking for the cause of what is popularly called 'labour welfare' that chiefly included the All India Trade Union Congress (Communist party of India), Hindu Mazdoor Sabha (Socialist Party), Bharatiya Mazdoor Sabha (Jana Sangha now BJP) and others. In this way, different political parties set their agenda for the cause of 'Labour Welfare' which led them to build up the industrial labour movements (interchangeably called the trade union movements) all over India inclusive of Assam. But so far as the tea industry of Assam and its workers called the TGLs, as noted above, are concerned the INTUC played the pioneering role in organizing and launching movements as well in the name of tea labour welfare. Their movements in Assam can, however, conveniently be divided into two parts on the periodical basis – (i) Colonial Phase (1826-1947) and (ii) Post-colonial phase (1947 - till today). The TGLs movements during the colonial era were organized neither at the state, district or local levels as well. They generally took place haphazardly on the tea estate wise and that took on a single given issue or demand. It happened primarily owing to the dearth of an organized tea trade union. In view of this, the present write-up is restricted to highlight the TGLs movement in the Brahmaputra valley of Assam in the post-colonial era only.

In this context, it would not be irrelevant to note that during the second part of the twentieth century a historical breakthrough took place in the TGLs movements of the state.

The brainchild developed by Mahendra Nath Sharma – the then General Secretary of the INTUC, Assam branch, contributed to restructuring and revitalizing the tea trade union with a common independent entity. Accordingly, a joint meeting of a galaxy of the then working as the district branches[4] of INTUC was convened on 9 August 1958 at Bordubi under the undivided North Lakhimpur district. The meeting unanimously resolved to form an integrated tea trade union comprising the working TGLs of the Brahmaputra valley called the Assam Chah Mazdoor Sangha with Robin Kakati, Mahendra Nath Sharma, and Jadunath Bhuyan as its President and Joint General Secretaries respectively. Since then the Assam Chah Mazdoor Sangha (hereinafter to be referred as the ACMS) officially affiliated to the INTUC has, in fact, been working as the Tea labour wing of the INC (I), in Assam. Its functional jurisdiction was decided to keep confined, as stated above, to the tea estates of the Brahmaputra valley with its head office in Dibrugarh town[5].

III

As mentioned above, the INTUC and later on ACMS that happened to be the tea trade union affiliated to the INC (I) party, were initially not required to build up anti-Government movement for the 'labour welfare'. Rather in many cases, the Government of India, as well as Assam, seemed to be sympathetic towards the TGLs particularly in the post-colonial era. This can be clear from the fact that the daily wage paid to the working TGLs constitute the mainstay of their livelihood and as such periodical enhancement of the same surfaced to be the most pressing demand for them. But the initiative in this direction came from the Government of India when it formulated the Minimum Wage Act in 1948 according to which the daily wage rate was hiked from Re 0.81 to Rs. 1.12[6]. This fixation of the TGLs daily wage, however, did not remain unaltered for the days ahead. Rather it went on rising. For instance, the Government of India set up a Wage Board in 1960 for the modification of TGLs daily wage rate. Based on the recommendation of the Wage Board, the Assam Tea Planters' Association, Jorhat, and the ACMS reached an agreement on 25 February 1966 to enhance the TGLs daily wage for a period of five years w.e.f. 1 January 1966 to 31 March 1970. While concluding the agreement both the parties unanimously resolved:

> *Under the present Excise Zone (which includes Assam Valley except Nowgong, Mangoldoi, Kamrup and Goalpara) for gardens over 150 acres will be increased as under – Men 16 paise, Women 13 paise, Children 8 paise, the wages with the above increase shall continue up to 31.03.1967 when on the basis of the average All India Consumers price index for the year 1966 the wages in all districts shall increase by 0.4 of a paise per point on increase over 170 increase and any one year*[7].

Like the earlier one, this fixation of TGLs daily wage did not remain static rather come under to further revision in the days to come. Of late, in this regard, an agreement was again reached between the ACMS and the *Consultative Committee for Planters' Association* (CCPA) on 4 February 2010. According to the agreement, the TGLs wage rate has been fixed at Rs. 66.50 in place of Rs. 58.50. Further, the agreement also decided to raise the wage on incremental basis i.e. Rs. 5.00 in the next year again Rs. 5.00 in the following year. In other words, their daily wage would ultimately go up to Rs. 76.50 in the upcoming two years[8].

Bonus (extra-gratuity paid to workmen) constitutes a potent source of enhancing the TGLs overall economic capability. Once the tea planters started making more and more surplus money out of tea plantation, they decided to award a minuscule portion of the same to the TGLs as well. As such for the first time the INTUC Assam Branch and the Tea Planters' Association held a series of dialogues that resulted eventually in signing a bilateral agreement pertaining to a bonus in 1956. Accordingly, the TGLs were paid Rs. 130/- per head as a bonus[9]. Thenceforth the payment of bonus to the TGLs has become mandatory and it is generally paid on the eve of Durga Puja festival every year that enables them to celebrate the same in a better way. Subsequently, the TGLs seemed to be unhappy with the lump sum bonus payment that forced the ACMS to take up the sensitive fiscal issue. Coming under the tremendous pressure of the ACMS, the tea planters' associations named the Assam Branch, Indian Tea Association (ABITA) came forward to sign an agreement on the bonus issue in 1975. In pursuance of the agreement, the minimum rate of the bonus was fixed at Rs. 8.33 percent and maximum Rs. 20 percent of the total income of a TGL in a given fiscal year. Nonetheless, over the past few years, the tea planters seemed to have been reluctant to pay bonus at the maximum rate on the pretext of the allegedly declining price of the finished tea product in the global market. Consequently, a few untoward incidents centering on the bonus issue seemed to have taken place in certain tea estates especially on the eve of widely celebrated Durga Puja festival among in TGLs and Ex-TGLs. The situation had even gone to the extent of labour casualty at the hands of the police and Para-military forces that were a scene. For such a situation the ordinary TGLs accused not only of the tea planters but the ACMS leadership as well for hopelessly being a failure to subside the most contentious bonus issue. Furthermore, the general TGLs even seemed to have alleged that the growing ACMS-Management nexus is chiefly accountable for making the ACMS incapable of fixing a uniform rate of bonus for all the TGLs working in various tea estates under its organizational jurisdiction. By and large, the TGLs bonus issue has been a critical day by day.

As a part of the social movement the INTUC, the predecessor of the ACMS, undertook a lot of innovative measures with a view to ameliorating the socio-economic and cultural backwardness of the TGLs women at large. The establishment of the Dibrugarh Chah Mazdoor Kalyan Samaj in 1956, inter alia, under the active initiative of Dalbirsingh Lohar, is a glaring venture in this direction. It is, in fact, a non-governmental organization committed to the cause of making TGLs woman economically self-reliant by way of imparting training for weaving and other technical know-how. Such training and technical know-how imparted have reportedly enabled a good number of TGLs women to get themselves self-employed for a dignified living[10].

IV

The ACMS happened to be equally concerned regarding the lingo-cultural development of the TGLs. They were of the firm opinion that the cultivation, advancement as well as the preservation of their colourful lingo-cultural heritage would help them accelerate the pace of their overall development. Keeping such a view in mind, on 6 August 1974 while submitting a memorandum to the Director General of the All India Radio (AIR), Delhi, the ACMS urged him to initiate a regular programme to broadcast the TGLs' colourful culture and heritage. Responding their urge in a positive way, the Central Government decided to introduce an AIR programme titled 'Chah Mazdoor Achor' *wef.* 6 April 1975 initially once a week on every Sunday evening for half an hour duration. Subsequently, this programme has been extended from once to thrice a week. Likewise in this context, two Assamese feature films named Ratanlal (1975) and Kechahoon (1985) reflecting the manifold socio-cultural dimensions of the TGLs life sponsored and produced by the ACMS is literally worth praising. In addition, the ACMS also undertook a fresh venture of publishing a monthly Assamese newspaper entitled Chah Mazdoor at a minimal price of Re one per copy since as far back as 1969. It has, genuinely speaking, been acting as the mouthpiece of the ACMS that renders ample opportunities for the growing TGLs boys and girls to expose and flourish their intellectual genius. Its publication from the ACMS Head Office (Dibrugarh) currently under the editorship of Trailukya Keot is still continuing. In the similar vein, the ACMS has, of late, published a number of books which chiefly include Robin Kakoty's, Gandhi, Asom Aru Asom Chah Mazdoor Sangha

(1989); Bishnulal Upadhyay's (ed) Swadhinata Sangrami Shramik Neta Dalbirsing Lohar (1993); Sushila Rajbonshi's Kechahoon (2006); Prahlad Tasa's Chah Bagichat Shikhyar Prachar (2005) and Chah Bagichat Gana Sakhyarata (2005); Hema Prova Tasa's Jibon Nadir Ghatat and Ardha Akash; Mancharam Patwari's Bharatiya Shramik Andolon, Bilateral Agreement (between Assam Chah Mazdoor Sangha and All Employers Association up to 10th April, 2006) and others. By and large, the literary movement built up by the ACMS has obviously contributed not only towards the enrichment of the world of Assamese language and literature but also generating awareness among the emerging TGLs youths.

As an integral part of their organized movement for socioeconomic elevation was the movement for the inclusion of the TGLs community into the Scheduled Tribes (ST) list of the Indian Constitution. Like the All Assam Tea Tribes Students' Association (1947) the ACMS, of late, perceived the necessity of the ST status for the TGLs. Indeed, their leadership was the firm conviction that the diametrical backwardness of their community could not be erased and eradicated unless they were equipped with the constitutional status of the Scheduled Tribes that ascertain extraordinary safeguards for development. As such in its plenary session held at Golaghat as far back as 1970 the ACMS unanimously passed a resolution urging upon the Government of India to treat or count all the people living in tea and ex-tea gardens as Scheduled Tribes irrespective of their caste or creed as they are in their states of origin. Likewise in order to reinforce their common demand the ACMS and Adivasi Council of Assam (ACA) jointly submitted a memorandum to the Prime Minister of India and the then members of both the Houses of Parliament on 15 July 1980 in which they repeatedly pleaded:

> *The Adivasis of Assam comprising various castes and tribes are recognized as Scheduled Tribes and Scheduled Castes in their states of origin such as Orissa, Bihar, Madhya Pradesh, Andhra Pradesh, West Bengal etc. but*

in the state of Assam they were not scheduled. The question of scheduling immigrant castes and Tribes/ Labourers of Tea and Ex-tea Gardens of Assam was taken up in the past by various Commissions and Committees appointed by the Government of India and all such bodies have opined that these Castes and Tribes were quite backward socially, educationally and economically, even then the local leaders were consistently opposing their inclusion in the State list of Scheduled Tribes and as such they have until today not made any significant progress to merge themselves with the mainstream of our National Life[11].

Notwithstanding the ACMS has not been successful in getting one of their most pressing demands of scheduling fulfilled till today and as such the same remains lingering.

V

Since the ACMS, as discussed above, is inextricably intertwined with the INTUC, affiliated to the Indian National Congress (now Congress (I) party) it obviously got involved in the electoral politics right from the days of its inception. In other words, the ACMS leadership were of a deep-seated belief that the involvement of theirs into the electoral politics of the state[12] on the basis of reciprocal understanding was the most effective means of ensuring 'their security and development by way of enactment of law'. The INC party, on the other hand, conceived it prudent to mobilize the TGLs under the banner of a trade union, what is called the ACMS, in order to garner their support enmass and thereafter to wrest political power and perpetuate the same in the state. The INC party, therefore, on the eve of every general election to the Assam Legislative Assembly (ALA) seemed to be sympathetic towards the ACMS demands more specifically while nominating candidates to fight election from different Tea and Ex-Tea people concentrated constituencies. It may be evident from the fact that the ACMS leader of Dibrugarh Branch named Dalbirsing Lohar was twice elected to the ALA as the Congress candidate backed by the TGLs from Saikhowa (1946) and

Tinsukia Constituency (1952). Similarly Sanu Kheria, the founder president of Golaghat Branch, ACMS was elected to the ALA as the Congress nominee in 1967 election followed by Chitra Gopal Karmakar (Sarupathar), Moliya Tanti (Doomdooma) and Upen Sanatan (Chabua) constituencies respectively. Thus a host of the ACMS, as well as non-ACMS sponsored leaders belonging to both the TGLs and non-TGLs communities, got elected to the ALA as a vibrant means of bringing about progress and prosperity of the TGLs at large. They chiefly included Bijoy Chandra Bhagawati, Kamakhya Prasad Tripathy, Biswadev Sharma, Jagannath Bhuyan, Durgeswar Saikia, Moliya Tanti, Upendranath Sanatan, Dipak Murmu, and Rameshwar Dhanowar, Gojen Tanti, Chitra Gopal Karmakar, Bishnulal Upadhyay, Narendranath Sharma, Mohikanta Das, Lily Sengupta and many others. Chitra Gopal Karmakar happened to be the first TGLs legislator inducted into the Council of Ministers in the capacity of Minister of State for labour. Likewise, Gojen Tanti from Mariani constituency happened to be the first Cabinet Minister of the TGLs Community with the portfolio of Labour and Supply.

In this way, it seemed that there has been an escalating scramble among the politically ambitious TGLs leaders to occupy the topmost office in the ACMS or its branches as a means of bargaining with the INC party for nomination to contest election with TGLs enblock backing. This can be substantiated by the electoral picture of a number of ALA constituencies where a host of the ACMS-backed TGLs and Ex-TGLs leaders fought the election of 1985 onwards as the INC (I) candidates[13].

	Nos. of Constituency	Candidate	Pol. Party	Result
1	Ratabari	Kumari Rabidas	INC (I)	Elected
2	Patharkandi	Monilal Gowala	-do-	-do-
28	Gossaigaon	Mithius Tudu	-do-	-do-
13	Lakhipur	Dinesh Prasad Gowala	-do-	-do-
70	Majbat	Silvious Condopan	-do-	-do-
123	Digboi	Rameswar Dhanowar	-do-	-do-

125	Doomdooma	Dileswar Tanti	-do-	-do-
89	Kaliabor	Boloram Nag	INC (I)	Defeated
94	Sarupothar	Arklius Tirkey	-do-	-do-
100	Titabor	Rupam Kurmi	-do-	-do-
105	Mahmora	Narad Kumar	-do-	-do-
106	Sonari	Satya Tanti	-do-	-do-
117	Lahowal	Dipak Murmu	-do-	-do-
119	TingKhong	Paban Singh Ghatowar	-do-	-do-
121	Chabua	Upen Sanatan	-do-	-do-

This trend nonetheless, continued to be increasing in the subsequent elections that led the INC (I) State Branch to accommodate as far as possible more ACMS-supported TGLs and Ex-TGLs candidates as its nominees in order to ensure their winning prospect bright and thereby perpetuate power in the State politics. Thus, the ACMS has, virtually speaking, acquired the incredible capacity to influence the INC (I) party and played a decisive role in the contemporary State's electoral politics. On the whole, the ACMS representing the TGLs and Ex-TGLs got itself converted into an INC (I) Tea cell 'a traditional supporter of the Congress party ... are continuously supporting the Congress party in Assam'[14]. This became clear while submitting a memorandum to the Congress High Command, Mrs. Sonia Gandhi on 20 December 2000 in New Delhi the ACMS President Mr. Paban Singh Ghatowar categorically maintained:

> *Tea and Ex-Tea Tribes community known as the Tea and Ex-Tea Labour Community had been brought by the Britishers more than 150 years ago to engage them as labourers in tea plantation of Assam. They are now part and parcel of Assam and Assamese society and are a traditional supporter of Indian National Congress. It is needless to say that the Tea and Ex-Tea Garden Labour voters are continuously supporting the Congress party in Assam. There are a number of instances when other people left the Congress Party, this population remained intact in support of the Congress Party. The whole tea population cannot think of any other ideology other than the Congress*[15].

Most probably this is the reason for which currently there are altogether ten TGLs members in the ALA[16] and out of them, seven won elected as the ACMS-sponsored Congress candidates. Thus coming under the pressure of the ACMS, the INC (I) party was forced to accord substantial weight to the TGLs and Ex-TGLs community specifically while nominating candidates for the electoral fight as well as forming Ministry also so as to keep their support for the Congress party intact. Notwithstanding the TGLs leadership, of late, seemed to be discontent with the strength of representatives they are having in the ALA so far. What they genuinely want is more representation in the ALA which it is perceived, they deserve[17]. While justifying more representation in a memorandum submitted to Mrs. Sonia Gandhi, the All India Congress Committee (AICC) Chairperson on 10 December 2000 Mr. Paban Singh Ghatowar forcefully pleaded:

> *Tea and Ex-Tea population dominated as many as 35 Assembly seats directly and 15 Assembly seats indirectly as deciding factor. Secondly, at the time of Lok Sabha election, the Tea and Ex-Tea Tribes community are the determining factor for the Congress candidates in as many as seven Lok Sabha seats. They are Dibrugarh, Jorhat, Koliabor, Tezpur, Mongoldoi, Silchar and Karimganj. But according to the population of Tea and Ex-Tea Tribes Community, the representation is not sufficient in Legislative Assembly, Lok Sabha, and Rajya Sabha. With the growing political awareness in this community, a feeling has already developed among them at the time of finalization of party nominations. We are under heavy pressure from our community to apprise you of their feeling and request you to examine this matter and take corrective steps to improve the situation and this makes our people feel that the AICC under your leadership is sympathetic to our cause*[18].

Perhaps coming under the influence of the ACMS, the Tea Cell of the Assam Provincial Congress Committee (APCC) also demanded 35 ALA constituencies be reserved for the

TGLs and Ex-TGLs Community[19] so as to ensure their adequate representation and ventilation of grievances in the proper forum for smooth redressal. Similarly, the All Tea Tribes Students' Association (1947) and All Adivasi Students Association of Assam (1996) - the two TGLs and Adivasis (those who prefer to identify as the Adivasis whose place of origin is the same with that of the TGLs and Ex-TGLs) organizations too had expressed a profound sense of regret that their community had not been assigned due share by political parties in the event of nominating candidates to fight elections. They accused the parties of being marginalized them in this context and therefore, decided to forge a political party on the basis of consensus to be evolved among their leaders associated with various parties to contest elections under separate banner but yet not done.

VI

From the foregoing discourse, it can clearly be comprehended that the ACMS, ever since its inception, has been successful in building up a vibrant social movement basically based on twin objectives, viz. the socio-economic and political ones. Firstly the ACMS made an appearance as the messiah of the hapless TGLs who remained impoverished, backward and disorganized for a long. In view of this, the ACMS leadership had to spearhead agitational phases, when required, demanding the enhancement of daily wage and other material facilities for the TGLs leading to the signing of a bilateral agreement with the Tea Planters Association on the basis of giving and take policy. In addition, it was found that the ACMS started intensifying its jurisdiction of activities from socioeconomic to culture-literary upliftment of both the TGLs as well as Ex-TGLs. More importantly, the ACMS by birth itself is, as mentioned elsewhere, connected with the Indian National Congress as its labour wing capacity. As such the ACMS is to muster the en bloc support of the TGLs and Ex-TGLs in order to ascertain the INC (I) victory in the game of power politics. While doing so, the budding enlightened elite belonging to the TGLs and Ex-TGLs also started to get themselves associated with the ACMS and its branches in a bid to build up their future political career. Consequently, in due course, a host of TGLs and Ex-TGLs leaders got elected to the ALA and Parliament as the INC (I) nominees strongly sponsored by the ACMS. In other words, the ACMS has virtually been a suitable platform to build up the political career of the politically ambitious TGLs and Ex-TGLs leaders. As such, there has been a scramble among the political aspirants to occupy prominent portfolios either of the ACMS or its branches as effective means of justifying their claim for the INC (I) nomination to fight the election that provides them an opportunity if elected to serve their community. Of course, while projecting the overall interest of the TGLs and Ex-TGLs community, some quarters of theirs seemed to have seriously complained that the personal and party interests are accorded more weight than the former. Despite so, it is an undeniable fact that the ACMS could be credited with generating and inculcating fresh awareness among the TGLs and Ex-TGLs that has manifested in various sorts of social movements carried out so far under its able leadership successfully or sometimes partially successfully.

Notes

1. Ghanashyam Shah, *Social Movements in India: A Review of the Literature*, Sage Publications, New Delhi, 1990, pp. 183.
2. In this context, it is worthwhile to mention that in the post World War I the labour (working) class movement in India acquired the organized form that culminated in the foundation of trade unions. Prior to it, a plethora of labour movements took place in unorganized and spontaneous ways in which leadership emerged from within the labour class. Subsequently, leadership began to emanate from outside as the philanthropic. Thus in the post-colonial era the industrial labour class movement, the leadership nature had undergone a metamorphosis which resulted in the involvement of an educated non-labour leader of political parties (Ghanashyam Shah, ibid, pp. 196-201).
3. It may be noted that the first tea labour union in the Brahmaputra Valley was founded in 1945 in Sibsagar under the stewardship of

Mr. P.M.Sarwan- a Christian enlightened member of the TGLs Community. Mr. Sarwan categorically disclosed his commitment towards the TGLs well-being and as such, he worked in collaboration with the colonial tea planters (Amalendu Guha, *Planter Raj to Swaraj: Freedom Struggle and Electoral Politics in Assam 1826-1947*, New Delhi, 1977, pp. 193).

4. These branches included (i) Dibrugarh Zila Chah Mazdoor Sangha, (ii) Sibsagar Zila Chah Mazdoor Sangha (iii) Jorhat Zila Chah Mazdoor Sangha (iv) Tezpur Zila Chah Mazdoor Sangha (v) Lakhimpur Zila Chah Mazdoor Sangha (vi) Mongoldoi Zila Chah Mazdoor Sangha (vii) Golaghat Zila Chah Mazdoor Sangha.
5. PS. Ghatwar, 'A brief account of the activities of the Assam Chah Mazdoor Sangha for 1986-88' appeared in the Souvenir of the 8th National Conference, Indian National Plantation Worker's Federation, Silchar, 28-30 January 1989.
6. Debendranath Bordoloi, 'Asomot Chah Mazdoor Sanghar Itihaas', *Eti Koli Duti Paat*, Souvenir of the ACMS Silver Jubilee Conference held at Dibrugarh on 14-15 February 2009, pp. 23-24.
7. Bilateral Agreements between Assam Chah Mazdoor Sangha and All Employers Association up to 16th June 1997 (compiled by the ACMS, affiliated to INTUC, Central Office, Dibrugarh, Assam, pp. 2-3).
8. Reported in the Amar Asom (Assamese daily) 5 February 2010.
9. Demand for the bonus payment was first raised by two veteran trade union leaders named Mr. Mahendra Nath Sharma and Mr. Kamalaprasad Tripathy in 1954 on the ground of making an unprecedented profit by the tea planters. Due to their persistent pressure, the tea planters introduced bonus in 1956 (Golok Sharma, *Modendranath Sharma Aru Shramik Andolon*, Souvenir, INTUC Assam Branch 22 August 1988, pp. 21).
10. Bijoy Chandra Bhagawati, *Moor Moromor Sanmanita Sahakarmi Lohar*, appeared in Bishnulal Upadhyay's (Ed) *Swadhinata Sangrami Shramik Neta Dalbir Singh Lohar*, Chah Mazdoor Bhawan, Dibrugarh, 1993, pp. 7-9.
11. Memorandum submitted to the Honourable Mrs. Indira Gandhi, Prime Minister of India, New Delhi on 15 July 1980 jointly by the Assam Chah Mazdoor Sangha, Adivasi Council of Assam, Assam, Tea and Ex-Tea Garden Tribes Youth Association and Tea and Ex-Tea Tribes MPs and MLAs.
12. In this context is worth mentioning that during the colonial era the tea and ex-tea Advisasis were scheduled as Tea Garden Coolie

tribes and they were represented by four nominated members by the Assam Legislature during the Sadullah Ministry in 1937 and they included Mr. P. Paridha (Silchar, Cachar) Mr. Bidesi Pantany (Doomdooma, Lakhimpur) and Mr. Binod Kumar Sarwan (Thakurbari, Darrang). Memorandum submitted to the Secretary-General, Lok Sabha, New Delhi by the ACMS and ACA on 9 September 1978.

13. Report on the Eighth General Election to the Assam Legislative Assembly and the House of People, 1985, Election Department of Assam.
14. Memorandum presented to Mrs. Sonia Gandhi, the President of the All India Congress Committee by a group of Assam's MLA belonging to the TGLs under the stewardship of Mr. Paban Singh Ghatowar, the President of the ACMS and Ex-Union Minister, New Delhi on 20 December 2000.
15. *Ibid.*
16. Name of the Congress MLAs representing TGLs and Ex-TGLs Community who got elected in the 2006 general election included: Durga Bhumij (Doomdooma). Rameswar Dhanowar (Digboi), Raju Sahu (Chabua), Prithvi Majhi (Lahowal), Jibontara Ghatowar (Moran), Rupjyoti Kurmi (Mariani), Dinesh Prasad Gowala (Lakhimpur) and Silvius Condopan (Dhakiajuli). The lone BJP MLA of TGLs Community was Rameswar Teli (Duliajan).
17. Reported in the Amar Asom (Assamese daily) Guwahati, 13 November 2000
18. The memorandum submitted to Mrs. Sonia Gandhi, op.cit
19 The ALA constituencies demanded by the ACMS and APCC Tea Cell to be reserved for the TGLs and Ex-TGLs Community include : (i) Patharkandi (ii) Udarband (iii) Gossaigaon (iv) Lakhipur (v) Bodsola (vi) Paneri (vii) Dhekiajuli (viii) Ratabari (ix) Majbat (x) Gohpur (xi) Behali (xii) Biswanath Chariali (xiii) Rangapara (xiv) Kaliabor (xv) Sarupothar (xvi) Bokakhat (xvii) Khumtai (xviii) Mariani (xix) Titabor (xx) Teok (xxi) Nazira (xxii) Sonari (xxviii) Mahmora (xxiv) Thowra (xxv) Moran (xxvi) Tingkhong (xxvii) Naharkatia (xxviii) Duliajan (xxix) Tinsukia (xxx) Digboi (xxxi) Doomdooma (xxxvii) Sadiya (xxxiii) Lahowal (xxxiv) Margherita (xxxv) Chabua (Reported in the Dainik Janambhumi, 9 January 2006).

CHAPTER - 5

ZELIANGRONG MOVEMENT IN THE CONTEXT OF SOCIAL CHANGE AND DEVELOPMENT IN NAGA SOCIETY

CHURA GIRI

The social movement has become an important theme of investigations for researchers. As the social movement involves varieties of social factors, the researchers have been getting interested in the study of social movement with an objective of social change and development through such movement. International Encyclopaedia of social sciences defines a social movement as 'a variety of collective attempts to bring about change. The attempts may be to bring in the certain social institution and to create an entirely new social order. Or the attempts may represent a socially shared demand for change in some aspects of the social order'. Wilkinson (1971) pointed out that the language ideas and styles of movement inevitably reflect wider cultural changes and can often be found to be important in themselves as agencies of cultural change. A social movement has, therefore, important expressive and aesthetic dimensions revealing both cultural distinctiveness and assimilatory tendencies in the wider society. Turner and Kilhan (1987) define a social movement as a collectively which acts with some continuity to promote or resist change in the society or group of which it is a part. Toch (1965) emphasizes that a social movement is an effect of a large number of people to solve collectively a problem they feel they share in common.

Having considered social movement, in general, we may attempt to discuss a movement like Zeliangrong in India, in general, and in the Northeastern region of India in particular, Movements emerged as a great harbinger of social change and development. One such movement is the Zeliagrong movement which spreads over parts of Manipur, Nagaland, and Assam. Nagaland is the pivotal ground of this movement. It is noteworthy that the tribals have fought more than hundred recorded battles against British led by heroes like Alluri Sitaram Raju, Birsa Munda, Sidho, Kanho Chand, Tilaka Majhi, Bhairon, Pashi Raja and Rani Gaidinliu without exception, all of them had to resist the onslaught of Christian missionaries too as the battle against the British also meant battling to safeguard their religions.

Rani Gaidinliu of Nagaland had led a heroic guerrilla war against the British and when defeated by the mightier British army was rewarded life imprisonment by means of a fair trial when she was the just tender age of sixteen. Pt. Jawahar Lal Nehru met her in Kohima jail and wrote poetically about her heroism calling her fit to be a Rani, hence the title of Rani. After the independence of India, it took Nehru more than one year to see her out of jail. Srimati Indira Gandhi awarded her the Padma Bhushan and also a Tamra Patra in the silver jubilee year of Independence Day, But Kohima church and the Christian leaders of the NSCN opposed vehemently when there was a proposal to have her statue installed in Kohima after her death because she had declared her Hereka and Zeliangrong movement Hindu and had refused to convert Christianity. Hereka School at Tenning is the burning example of her courage and resist against conversion. So, we have considered this social movement in the form of socio-religious politico reform movement which was first launched by Jodanang in the late 1920s and later led by Rani Gaidinliu in the North West hills of Manipur.

Haipou Jodanang who initiated this uprising was a Kabui Naga. His aim was to unite three constituents of Naga tribes; the Zemeis, Liangmeis, and Rongmeis (Zeliangrong) to drive away the British as well as Kukis who were regarded as outsiders. Jadonang was supposed to have the powers of a 'sorcerer' and the Kacha Nagas 'believing that he is the 'Messiah' for whom they have been waiting for sent him a large number of Mithun's and domesticated *gayals* as tributes .'The objective of the uprising was a 'socio-religious reformation and political goal to separate the Zeliangrong from the British regime. And his aim was to establish Naga Raj.' But before achieving his goal he was implicated and sentenced to death on 13th June 1931. After his execution, Gaidinliu, a young unmarried girl of only 17 years old carried the movement by organizing armed rebellion which was also suppressed in 1932. Jadonang and Gaidinliu called on the people to disobey the oppressive laws of the British regime and not to pay house tax.

Jadonang's religious ideas were crystallized in the 'Heraka cult' by Gaidinliu who was regarded as his 'spiritual successor.' Gaidinliu was wanted on the charge of murder and arrested in September 1932. The 'Heraka Cult' which was revived by Gaidinliu spread over a large area of Naga Hills, Manipur and the North Cachar Hills. Her capture saved a situation of the grave danger of a serious outbreak. But finally, she was sentenced to life imprisonment. She was released after 1947 by the Government of India which acknowledged her as a patriotic freedom fighter. The late Prime Minister Jawaharlal Nehru referred to her as Rani. Since then she came to be known as Rani Gaidinliu, and she was recognized as a political sufferer, awarded pension. But it has been argued that she did not fight for the Indian freedom struggle. Moreover, none of the Nagas participated in the Indian National Congress which led to the Indian freedom struggle. Gaidinliu, in fact, fought for the unification of Zeliangrong freedom from foreign rule, reform the practice of Heraka Cult and to establish the Naga Raj'

Origin and History of the 'Naga'

Before the advent of the British into the Naga Hills, the inhabitants of these hills knew themselves by the designation of their respective tribes only. The name, however, was not in general use among the Nagas. It was in the last century after the occupation of some parts of the particular hill range, that the British colonialist called the hill areas as Naga Hills, and then onwards the term 'Naga' began to be widely used for all these tribes who settled in this range.

There are various theories about the origin of the word 'Naga' and there is no unanimity of the opinion. In spite of the different theories regarding the origin of the term 'Naga, however, there is a consensus that the word 'Naga' is given to particular tribes by the Aryan-speaking people to mean naked hill people. It is a fact that the word 'Naga' remained a terror to the Aryan-speaking Assamese for ages. To them, it was understood to mean naked 'Hill Men or a headhunter'.

Ptolemy, the Greek scholar in his Geographia had mentioned the words 'Naga log' which means the realm of the naked people in about 150 A. D., interestingly, the location which Ptolemy described the naked people has been the exact place in which the present Nagas are living now.

Another theory is that the word 'Naga' originated from the word 'Nag' meaning 'snake'. A further theory attributed to J. H. Hutton suggests that the word 'Naga' originally was a corruption of the Assamese word 'Noga' probably meaning a mountaineer. It is merely a European lengthening of Assamese word Noga (pronounced Naga).

According to Captain Butler, 'the term Naga is derived from the word 'naga' meaning 'naked' crude and barbarous. W. Robinson also suggested some related theories of the origin of the word 'Naga'. He writes that 'the origin of the word is unknown, but it has been supposed by some to have been derived from the Sanskrit word 'Nagna' and applied in derision to the people, from the paucity of their clothing. but there seems a little foundation for this etymological derivation as the term has never been known to be applied by the Bengalese to either to the Khasis or the Garos with whom they were far better acquainted than with the Nagas; and besides, the Garos are habitually accustomed to a greater degree of nudity than any of the Naga tribes with whom we are acquainted with.'

The collective designation of the origin of the word 'Naga' writes E. A. Gait by which the Nagas are known to the Assamese seems to be derived as suggested by Holcombe and Peal from 'Nok' which means 'folk' in some of the tribal dialects (Nok or Noka means people). He suggested that there was some connection between this and the Sanskrit 'Noka'. The Burmese also called 'Na-ka' which means people with pierced ears.' The word 'Naga 'is said to be another form of 'Na-ka' as the Nagas both man and woman pierced their ears.'

Verrier Elwin suggests that the probability of the origin of the word Naga from the word 'Nok' or people which are its meaning in a few Tibeto-Burman languages as in Garo, Nocte, and Ao

The origin of the word Naga is still a mystery. It is highly possible that the word Naga is given by the Assamese, Bengalis, and Burmese. It can also be assumed that the term Naga is generally defined as a political construct and as a cultural abstraction. Though the origin of the term Naga is obscured some would say it was given by others and possibly means no more than 'people' or 'warrior'. Each Naga tribe has its own name. Thus the Tenyima are known as Angami, the Sumis as Sema, the Ao as Metikumi or Aor, the Sangtam as Lophomi, the Konyak as Taprongumi and so on. The present nomenclatures were probably coined by the British. The different tribes speak their own Tibeto-Burman dialects and use Nagamese or English, Nagaland's official language as their lingua franca.

Thus micro – identities remain rooted, but there has been a trend towards larger groupings of neighbouring tribes with shared traditions or other similarities have come together.

This is illustrated by the use of acronyms to describe the new group formations. Thus the Zemis Langmei and Rongmei came together in 1974 as the Zeliangrong, brought together by adherence to the Hinduised Hereka cult preached by Jadonang whose disciple, Rani Gaidinliu, later rose to fame for defying the Raj. Similarly, the Chakrhu, Kheza, and Sangtam formed the Chakesang. The Pochury, in turn, are Nagas from the three villages of Sapo, Kechui, and Khury.

Nagaland is the pivotal ground of this movement. The field of study is chosen in the bulky inhabitation of Zeliangrong Nagas in Nagaland. Assam, another germination ground of movement is also selected for the study. Assam is one of the states of the northeastern region of India. Assam has thirty-two districts. Amongst the two hill districts namely Dima Hasao and Karbi Anglong and the adjacent part of Tinsukia district to Arunachal Pradesh are the inhabitations of Naga tribes. Nagaland is dominated by 86.50 percent (census, 2011) of tribal. The main inhabitant of Nagaland is the Nagas, an Indo –Mongoloid people. Naga itself is a generic term for a cluster of thirty-two tribes, of which five in Myanmar, sixteen tribes are scattered in all seven districts of Nagaland, Karbi Anglong and Tinsukia district of Assam. Three Naga tribes - the Zemis of N.C. Hills of Assam and Nagaland, the Langmei, and Rongmei who are found both in Cachar and Manipur, together constitute the Zeliangrong group. They are closely akin to each other and spread over three states of the northeastern region of India, such as Manipur, Nagaland, and Assam, and have merged their identities to revive their traditional religion and to make it more specific.

We attempt to discuss the Zaliangrong movement as a socio-religious and political movement led by Rani Gaidinliu. The data for this chapter collected through case studies, observation historical methods. An in-depth interview is taken from the respondents those who witnessed the movement. Besides primary data, secondary data are also used for this chapter.

In the first part of the twentieth century, a movement was launched in the whole country against the foreign rule. Though the Britishers tried to stop it from entering the hilly region of Northeast India and introduced the Inner Line Regulation; even then the movement somehow or other entered the Naga Hills. The Nagas tried in their own way to protect their religion, culture, and administration. Ultimately, other tribes admitted the British supremacy over them but the Zeliangrong people did not submit. Though the Zeliangrong people were not fully aware of the Indian freedom movement, still they were influenced by it. They went on fighting against foreign culture and administration under the guidance and leadership of a Rani Gaidinliu. At the tender age of thirteen, she became associated with the movement started by one Jadonang, who belonged to her own clan. Within a short period, Jadonang collected hundreds of followers from his own tribe. Jadonang found that the traditional Zeliangrong religious practices prevented the people not only from social activities with heavy demand for material sacrifices but also were enslaved by the old religious rituals, taboos, and *gennas.* He devised a process of reformation of the old religious practices mainly for the purpose of strengthening the ultimate aim of wresting the political power from the hands of the alien rulers. He launched this movement since 1925 onwards and within six years he won the allegiance of the entire Zeliangrong people, stretching from Manipur through Naga Hills to North Cachar Hills and they gave full support to his call for the liberation of the Zeliangrongs. He sent his followers in all directions to preach about his liberation movement. His cousin Gaidinliu was made priestess and sent to Bhuban cave in North Cachar Hills. She was warmly received by her people there. About 10,300 followers were with her.

He encouraged Gaidinliu to continue the movement and to establish 'a Zeliangrong Raj' for their people, Jadonang was hanged in Imphal on 29th August 1931, on a charge of making a human sacrifice.

By executing Jadonang, the British Government could not stop the movement. Rather Gaidinliu continued the movement more vigorously in the hills on a large scale.

In the meantime, Gaidinliu made some contact with some revolutionary nationalist leaders of Surma Valley to launch a large-scale revolutionary movement jointly. But it was not an easy task for them because the government kept a strict watch on the Gaidinliu movement.

The Zeliangrong people stopped paying taxes to the government. She started getting support from every nook and corner of the Zeliangrong territory. They refused to offer any kind of help to the alien rulers including labour and compulsory porterage. She became a living legend. The British government used all kinds of methods to spoil her growing charisma. Her followers treated her as a superhuman personality.

Under her leadership, the Zeliangrong people tried to over through the British administration and to start their own administration, they tried to overthrow a foreign religion and to establish their own religion in a reformed form and to protect their own customs and traditions. This resistance came from the crisis of identity. People were afraid of losing their identity seeing the assimilation process with western culture and administration. The Zeliangrong people were now united to protect their identity even at the cost of their lives.

When Gaidinliu was in jail some foreign Christian Missionaries visited her and requested her to convert herself to Christianity and tempted her that she would be released from jail and would be made Pastor if she converts. But they could not convince her.

When India attained her independence Gaidinliu was released from Tura jail in 1947. But she was not allowed even in free India to go back to her Zeliangrong inhabited area for a long time. After her release for some years, she had to live in Mokokchung. The government of India sanctioned a political pension for her in April 1959.

She met the central leaders and acquainted them with the problems of her people. When she realized that the center was not giving importance to her demands she revitalized the movement. In the meantime, the Naga underground movement led by the Naga National Council (NNC) in Nagaland and Manipur was in full action. So her efforts to unify the Zeliangrong people caused displeasure among them. The NNC started giving her troubles and the insurgents attempted her life even.

Ultimately she took arms in her hand in 1960 and went underground to protect her life and to defend their religion reformed by her. She raised an armed force of about 1000 followers and collected about 500 rifles. Her armed personnel clashed with the NNC rebels and killed many of them who were involved in activities against Zeliangrong movement. This second phase of her underground life lasted for six years. At the persuasion of the Deputy Commissioner of Kohima Mr. S.C. Deb, Rani Gaidinliu agreed to lay down arms and to work for the welfare of her Zeliangrong people incorporation with the Government through peaceful means. She came out from the jungle in January 1966 and later on she visited New Delhi and met the central leaders. She called on the Prime Minister Mrs.Indira Gandhi and demanded to create a separate administrative unit for the Zeliangrong people. Prime Minister agreed to take up speedy development activities and coordinated planning in the Zeliangrong areas of Manipur, Nagaland, and Assam.

In the meantime, during her stay in jail and in Mokokchung after her release, the Naga Christian missionaries extended their mission up to the Zeliangrong area. This way the Christian missionaries could enter the Zeliangrong area and the Christian missionaries spread some rumors against her and tried to convert her followers to Christianity. This way the Christian missionaries entered the Zeliangrong area.

Now only about 25 percent of the total Zeliangrong people follow the religion which she said a cult of Hinduism.

Now the Government is giving her a free furnished house, vehicle, telephone, bodyguards personal secretary and also a pension. Under her leadership, Herakame Leu the religion of the Zeliangrong people is well organized with a formal structure.

The traditional Zeliangrong religion believes in a Supreme Being called Tingwang Raguang or Tingwang who is the creator of the universe. He is benevolent. There is the belief in the existence of a heaven. The sinless souls go to heaven after death there is also a belief in the worship of nature which is a living phenomenon to the Zeliangrong deities representing different aspects of nature, for example, Fire God and others like water spirit, field spirit etc.

Besides they have village deity family deity and household deity. Ancestor worship is also prevalent in the traditional Zeliangrong religion. The main form of worship is also prevalent in the traditional Zeliangrong religion. The main forms of worship are offering of sacrifices and chanting of 'Ho'. There are other ceremonies like birth and death. In short, their traditional religion is polytheism.

Rani Gaidinliu tried to reform their traditional religion and to make it simpler. They now call this cult the Hereka Leu.'Hereka' in Zemi language means 'pure and 'Leu' means religion. The Heraka leu believes in Tingkao Reauang or Tingwang who is the creator of the universe. They do not worship smaller gods and goddesses, spirits and deities. This way they introduced monotheism in place of polytheism among the Zeliangrong people worship of ancestor spirits is also abolished. The modes of worship and birth and death writs are simplified. The great sacrifices of animals to Tingkao Raguan are still prevalent among them. The numerous *gennas* which are observed by the Zeliangrongs have abolished with a view to having more time for work.

The marriage ceremonies have been simplified and traditional bride price system has been abolished. Traditional village administration, customary law, youth dormitories for both boys and girls from other traditional village organizations are still maintained. They still perform their traditional festivals.

After interviewing the respondents the following factors are found to be responsible for its emergence;

1. Identity Crisis; Just after the First World War people in the remote areas were exposed to the outer world. They realized that they were going to lose their customs, traditions, religion etc. They also realized the importance of preserving their identity, which gave birth to this tribal movement.
2. The impact of Indian National movement; In the remote hills also people came to know about Indian national freedom movement beyond the inner line which encouraged them to fight for their independence.
3. Political Motive; Behind this socio-religious movement there was a political motive of establishing a Zeliangrong autonomous unit to be distinguished from other neighbouring Christian tribes.

When we consider the clash between NNC and Gaidinliu, the movement it reveals the following underlying causes;

1. Religion; The NNC was mainly confined within the Angamis and the Chakhesangs. These two tribes were converted to Christianity sometimes back. These Christians tribes were trying to convert the Zeliangrong people to Christianity. But Jadonang and Gaidinliu resisted it with the support of their followers.
2. Ideological Differences; While the NNC was trying to establish a new sovereign independent Nagaland comprising all the Naga inhabited areas of present

Nagaland, Manipur, Assam, Arunachal Pradesh and Burma including the Zeliangrong people the Rani was trying to establish a Zeliangrong an autonomous administrative unit within Indian union . The inner clash of ideology brought the armed clash between two groups.

3. Relationship with India; Rani Gaidinliu established a good relationship with the government of India which the underground and outlawed NNC could not tolerate.

While studying the attitude of the converted Christian Zeliangrong people it was known that they converted to Christianity because the traditional Zeliangrong religion in their opinion is very conservative and has no modern outlook. Even the traditional Zeliangrong religious leaders discouraged modern education system. On the other hand, the Christian religious leaders encouraged to adopt the modernization including modern education.

If the Rani and her colleagues would have possessed a modern outlook towards life, they could have resisted conversion to a large extent and could have retained their traditional culture.

References

Aosenba, 2001, *The Naga Resistance Movement, Prospects of Peace and Armed Conflict*, pp 2-3 and 24-25, Regency Publications; New Delhi.

Toch, H. 1965. *The Social Psychology of Social Movements.* Indianpolis, Ind: Bobbs-Merrill.

Turner, P and L. Kilhan, 1987. *Collective Behaviour*. NJ Prentice Hall; Englewood Cliffs

Verghese, BG, 1996, *India's Northeast Resurgent, Ethnicity, Insurgency Governance, Development*, pp 84, Konark Publishers; New Delhi.

Wilkinson, P. 1971. *Social Movement*. Wen Ching Publishers

CHAPTER - 6

REFLECTION ON ADIVASI MOVEMENT IN ASSAM

— — — — — —
PUSHPA CHAMPIA

This chapter attempts to present the chronology of the movements carried out by various Adivasi organizations in Assam and to bring to light the activities of various Adivasi organizations and their achievements. In Assam, the discovery of tea posed a challenge before the British tea Companies to establish the tea industry by recruiting labourers for the purpose of tea plantation. After initial experiments with the Chinese and Assamese labourers in particular apart from various other labourers, it was ultimately the labourers recruited from outside Assam, like- Bihar, Uttar Pradesh, Madhya Pradesh and Madras who fared as best labourers.

The entire population recruited for the tea gardens in Assam, gradually in the course of time came to be labeled as Tea garden coolie, Black tribal or Tea labourer[1]. Presently they are also branded as Tea tribes[2]. This terminology is coined by the amalgamation of diverse castes and tribes which speak different languages, practice different religions and customs. In spite of the fact that 'Tea tribe' enables the entire population which is around 70 lakhs today to be identified today under a single banner, a section of the tea garden working communities are unwilling to permit the hegemony of their professional identity to prevail over their tribal identity and instead prefer to be identified as 'Adivasi'. Apart from this, the Santhal colonies of west Assam (Gossaigaon subdivision) with a population of around 2 lakhs, provides ample evidence that Adivasis were not brought to Assam only for Tea Industries as Samuel Pando in his article 'Asomor Adivasi Asomiya Sokolok Chah Janajati Boolar Jukti Kot?' refers to the fact that some of these people were engaged by kings Naranarayana and Chilarai in 1546 in constructing the 'Gohain Komal Ali'. (*Agradoot*, 6th November 1996).

The word 'Adivasi' is, however, a generic term and it means the 'Indigenous' or the 'Original settlers' of India both in the North and in the South. But when we speak of the Adivasis in Assam, it requires greater analysis as Assam is a homeland of several tribes and ethnic groups from times immemorial and as such the situation is not identical as in any other part of India and as such 'it is not they, but some others (like Bodos, Kacharis etc.) who can more logically claim as Adivasi for the social group under study'[4].

It needs to be highlighted that these tribes in the tea gardens speak different languages among themselves though they speak one common language (*Sadri*) for communication. Just to mention a few tribes - Assur, Gond, Kondpan, Nagbhansi, Bhumij, Ho, Korwa, Oraon, Bhuyan, Karmakar, Kurmi, Parja, Bhil, Kharia, Lohra, Santal, Chik Baraik, Kisan, Majhi, Sawra, Ghatwal, Kol, Munda, Tanti etc.[5]

It is significant to mention that the Tea/Ex-Tea Garden workers/labourers were originally recognized as Scheduled Tribes/ Scheduled Castes prior to India's Independence but have been deprived of the scheduling benefits as they were not recognized as ST/SC immediately after India's Independence.[6]

The condition of the vast majority of the population of these labourers remains backward and deprivation of scheduling benefits appears to be one of the significant causes of this situation.

Although the entire tea garden population cannot be included under the 'Adivasi' banner, a section of the Adivasi opportunists for serving their political interests intends to include several castes groups also under its 'Adivasi' banner. The leaders holding such a view opine that castes groups are also included under the Adivasi banner, thereby would enable them to acquire better bargaining power.

Additionally the term 'Adivasi' cannot be accepted as appropriate terminology to encompass within its domain the vast tea garden working communities especially the several castes groups due to the fact that hegemony of tribe or tribal characteristics cannot prevail over the rest of the members of the community, yet the term Adivasi has acquired ample coverage in the recent times . The ethnic clashes in Kokrajhar in the year 1996, led to the formation of All Adivasi Students Association of Assam (AASAA) on the 2nd July 1996 and more importantly the Beltola incident on the 24th November 2007 in which an Adivasi girl was stripped in public, one casualty and hundreds injured led to widespread agitation of the Adivasi Movement in Assam.

However, a major chunk of the Adivasi population is in the Tea Gardens and is commonly labeled as Tea Tribes. Even after 62 years of our independence the plight and the situation of Adivasis in Assam, has been the same as in the pre-colonial days. In reality, they are considered as second class citizens of Assam. The development schemes almost never reach the tea garden areas. Education, health and livelihood programs of government are never implemented well in Adivasi inhabited areas. They are left in the hands of the tea garden companies whose policy is 'Low cost, high profit'. Today the Adivasi tea garden workers are living in sub-human conditions. The economic condition of the community is poor most of the ex-tea population is landless. Tea industry employees lakhs of workers but the political and social condition is very poor compared to other communities of Assam and also their literacy rate is much less compared to other communities.

These tribes[7] working in Assam tea gardens have been deprived of scheduled tribe status in the post-Independence era Although the Adivasis (tribes among the tea garden working for population) and the several caste groups in the tea garden working communities are socioeconomically much backward than all the other communities in Assam, it is very unfortunate that they are not included in their respective categories of S.T, or S.C. list, which can play a significant role in their upliftment.

Even in the post-colonial era, the Adivasi community is not free from the slavery of colonial planters. Adivasis along the years have organized themselves in various forms and have been fighting for their rights as Indian citizens. There arose various sociocultural, student and several other movements from the community over the years.

Some of the major Adivasi organizations are the Adivasi Council of Assam(1958), Chotnagpuria Chatra Sangha,(28th December 1947) which is now Assam Tea Tribe Student Association, All Adivasi Students' Association Of Assam(2nd July 1996), Assam Munda Mahasabha, All Assam Kurukh (Orang) Hongo, Munda Sahitya Sabha etc.

Adivasi Council of Assam (ACA): After independence Adivasis were mainly demanding for Scheduled Tribe status in Assam. Visit of Jaipal Singh Munda (MP) the 'Manrang Gomke' (chief leader or Head) in the month of March 1958, ignited the masses on scheduling issue (14th March 1958, *Hindustan Standard*). He said how the same constitution will differ for two brothers one at Assam and other in Bengal. Being the member of constitution drafting committee he knew that only political tactics will provide ST status to Adivasis. Therefore, Jaipal Singh Munda and Sushil Bage (MLA Bihar) visited Assam to organize people to demand ST status. During his visit, 1958 Adivasi Council of Assam was formed and meetings were held at several places under the leadership of Francis Hans, Bishal Topno of Lakhimpur and Simon Soren of Gossaigaon.

Chotnagpuria Chatra Sangha was formed under the leadership of Simon Singh Horo and Santosh Topno on 28th December 1947[8]. The same organization later came to be known as Assam Tea Tribe Student Association. Though initially there was no basic difference between ATTSA and All Adivasi Students Association of Assam (AASAA) later in the year 1996 a separate body of youth wing emerged out of basically the tea garden who had identified themselves as Adivasi. During 1984-85 it (ATTSA) lead a strong movement under the leadership of Lokeswar Kurmi (President) and Bhagirath Karan (Secretary). Their movement ended with an accord with AGP Government. According to understating, ATTSA got four AGP tickets for Assembly seats. All of the ATTSA leaders lost in the election. However, ATTSA created Tea Tribe identity which is not accepted by Experts. On 14th August 2006, Mr. Silvius Condapan raised the bill at parliament to include Adivasis in the ST list. Tribal Minister said that with regard to 97 communities, which are clubbed under one caption of tea tribes, the State Government has itself stated in its latest report that they do not have primitive traits and that they are not geographically isolated. The RGI has stated that they have furnished their comments four times - in the year 1978, 1981, 1995 and 2005 but he did not support the proposal because Assam Government sent the wrong report. In the year of 1985 central government was about to give Scheduled Tribe status to nine Adivasi tribes of Assam. But the then labour minister Barki Prasad Telga and ATTSA leader Mr. Bagirath Karan opposed and sent a resolution to Assam government to oppose the central government's move to grant Scheduled Tribes status only to nine tribes working in the tea garden and thus not recognizing the numerous other tribes as well as the castes in the tea garden in the SC/ST List as per their individual affiliation to the particular tribe/ caste. Struggle for Scheduling is still going on in several forms.

All Adivasi Student's Association of Assam (AASAA) was formed on 2nd July 1996 as a result of the ethnic clash of Kokrajhar. Initially, it worked well to solve the problems of

Adivasis. It was a strong organization from 1996 to 2003. For the first time, it was able to raise the demands of Adivasis at Delhi. Adivasi masses were able to lead strong movement demanding their rights from the government under the leadership of Justin Lakra of Gossaigaon (president), Joseph Minz of Lakhimpur (general secretary) and Bosco Chermako of Gossaigaon. Several leaders of AASAA sacrificed their life and are listed names in martyrs list by the community. Philemon Hemrom (Srirampur) sacrificed his life in police firing on 5th July 2000. Andrius Marandi Asst.General Secretary of AASAA gave his life at the gun of Bodo extremist on 8th March 2001. Eight Adivasis lost their lives in the police firing on 25th July 2002 during the *bandh* called by AASAA in demand of rehabilitation of Kakrajhar Adivasi IDPs and scheduling issue as well. They were *Jiten Tanti, Arun Tanti, Nathanial Munda, Dambu Hasa Purti, Sanika Sawasi, Mangra Mund and Basudeo Kherwar.* Hundreds of student were arrested and tortured whose names were not recorded.

Additionally, the movement led to the formation of organizations. All Adivasi Women's Association (AAWAA), Adivasi Sahitya Sabha (ASS) and many NGOs were formed to work for Adivasi Society. Several Adivasi Mahasabha were organized which took resolutions and plans to strengthen the community. A section of frustrated youth also started underground movement like Adivasi Security Force (ASF), Birsa Commando Force (BCF) Adivasi National Liberation Army (ANLA), and Adivasi Cobra Militant (ACM) which however is never supported by the people of the Adivasi community

The situation of Tea garden is deteriorating day by day. The extortion by extremist groups and other problems resulted in closing down of many tea gardens creating large-scale unemployment. The wage of the labourers is very low compared to labourers elsewhere. A Tea labourer gets a wage of about Rs70. There is high child labour in tea gardens. Lack of Education, health facilities, and Sanitation make tea

Labourers live in an inhuman condition. Sukumar Bogasi (*Asomor Arthaniti*, 1997) says that during their studies at several tea gardens they found that the labourers were living in sub-human conditions.

The Carnage of Kokrajhar and Adivasi IDPs

Ethnic conflict of 1996 displaced 2 lakh people and killed 8 thousand Adivasis[9]. 'Still Assam has a large number of Internally Displaced Persons (IDPs) including 33,362 persons in Kokrajhar district and 74,123 persons in Gossaigaon district' (India Human Right Report of 2006). They are some from forest area and some of them are Patta holders[10]. The government has not been able to rehabilitate the IDPs even after so many years. The pain and sufferings of Adivasis who are in the concentration camp of the government of Assam, living for last 15 years have compelled them to unitedly assert their demand along with the tribes of the tea gardens and demand for being scheduled in the S.T. list. More than one lakh people are still in the concentration camp (relief camp) of Kokrajhar District.

The Adivasis have also continued their struggle for several issues apart from asserting their demands for Scheduled Tribe status and it cannot be said that the community has not achieved anything. Continued movements have created mass awareness among the Adivasi population with regard to their identity. It may be mentioned that the different organizations like the Adivasi Council of Assam, Adivasi Sahitya Sabha, AASAA, All Adivasi Women Association of Assam (AAWAA) etc have been able to create awareness among the masses and create an identity as the Adivasis and although it is controversial it has been gaining wide currency.

The proposal of Adivasi Development Council' from the center for the upliftment of the Adivasis in Assam depicts a temporary solution to their long-standing demand. The council is still in its process of formation and if it implements its projects effectively, the Adivasi community might be able to acquire benefits out of its formation but whether it will be able to develop the Adivasi community only time can provide the answer.

Notes and References

1. 'Till the time of independence they were recognized as *Tea Garden Coolie Tribes* and they had accordingly nominated members of the provincial legislature... while accepting the status given by Jyoti Prasad Agarwalla in the absence of a universally acceptable term/name, we would prefer to call them *Black Tribals* of Assam mainly because this term specifies their racial traits, distinguishes them clearly from other Mongoloids- light yellow tribals and other groups of Assam. This term also signals the continuity of many aspects of their earlier tribal heritage and ways of life' (Monirul Hussain, *The Assam Movement: Class, Ideology and Identity,* Delhi, 1993, p. 184).
2. Coolie word was used to denote Adivasi Tea worker during and before 1950, Govt. records and Report like the Labour Inquiry Report of 1921, 1906 etc.
3. The President of the Adivasi Sahitya Sabha, Wilfred Topno, opines that Tea and Ex-Tea Tribes is used widely today, Govt. has opened Tea and Ex-Tea Tribe Directorate, whereas this type of department is not found in West Bengal and other tea cultivation state where Adivasi tribes are also working.
4. Bolin Hazarika: '*In Search of an Identity for an Ethnic Group: the Case of Tea and Ex-Tea Garden Labourers of Assam'* paper presented at the National Seminar on '*Ethnicity in Assam To-day*' held at the Centre for North- East Studies, Dibrugarh University on 12 and 13 March 2001.
5. The name was given by Assam Sahitya Sabha President during Patsala Conference of Assam Sahitya Sabha.
6. Memorandum to the select committee for Scheduling of Adivasis of Assam. On February 6, 1997 AASAA.p 6-7
7. A.K. Chanda Committee Report (Chairman of Scheduled Castes and Tribes (Amendment) Bill, 1967)
8. The list of the Adivasi tribes in the tea garden occupation has been mentioned in the Annexure- 111 of the Memorandum to the select committee for Scheduling of Adivasis of Assam, on February 6, 1997, AASAA.
9. Dineswar Tasa, *Kachasona,* Souvenir of ATTSA, Sonari 1983 (pp-79)

10. AASAA 'Memorandum to Prime Minister of India 2001.
11. Uddipana Goswami 'Internal displacement, migration, and policy in Northeastern India'. In the Adivasi IDP camps, however, there are as yet people who have *pattas* and have not been rehabilitated; even though they were official to be covered under the first phase of rehabilitation. (Goswami, 2006).

CHAPTER - 7

THE MOVEMENT FOR KUKI TRIBES AUTONOMOUS REGIONAL COUNCIL

L. DOUNGEL

Introduction

The demand for autonomy, regionalism, and statehood has become a common subject in India. The demand for autonomy stems from the sentiments people have towards a region, community or the tribe to which they belong. It is a manifestation of distinctiveness in respect of race, culture or language and also a concern to protect and preserve one's identity along with others, such as economic deprivations, suppression, domination, and neglect by the ruling majority. The Kukis demand for the autonomous regional council is no exception to this fact. India is a land of diversity the demands for autonomy and regionalism are not unexpected. In fact, anticipating this eventuality, the framers of our Constitution provided a framework for coping with such a situation and thereby attaining unity through sustaining diversity.

As indicated in the title, this article proposed to examine the political aspirations of the Kukis of Assam with special reference to the role played by the Kuki National Assembly (KNA) spearheading the movement for creation of a separate Kuki Tribes Autonomous Regional Council (KTARC) under the provisions of the Sixth Schedule to the Constitution of India, within the existing Karbi Anglong district of Assam.

Background

The political aspirations of the Kukis demanding for the creation of a separate autonomous regional council in Karbi Anglong district under the provisions of Sixth Schedule to the Constitution of India is unique and exceptional in so far as there are no other instances of such demand from the hill tribes of Assam, particularly in the post state-reorganization period. But in contrast, a number of autonomous councils have come up for different plain-tribal communities of Assam. All the same barring Boro Territorial Council, all of these Councils are basically functional in character without having any definite territorial jurisdiction. Thus, the KNA's demand for KTARC under the provision of Sixth Schedule to the Constitution is the only one of its kind justifiable and fittingly sanctioned by the law of the land.

It was in the early part of 1992 that the demand for Kuki Tribes Autonomous Regional Council (KTARC) by the Kukis of Karbi Anglong came into the limelight following the birth of Kuki National Assembly (KNA) spearheading the movement. The KNA thenceforth formally started submitting its representations and memoranda at various official and ministerial levels articulating its demands, expressing grievances and aspirations of the Kukis living in the district. But the movement was not vocal and popular compared to other political movements of its contemporary. It was actually overshadowed by relatively more organized and vociferous Autonomous State Demand Movement (ASDC) of the two hill districts of Karbi Anglong and Dima Hasao. The movement for KTARC also could not draw enough attention to the media and people at large particularly owing to the fact that the movement was committed to fulfilling its legitimate demand through democratic and constitutional means. The KNA therefore categorically avoided illegal and unlawful methods of pressing their demands to draw the necessary attention of the concerned authorities. It restrained itself from adopting a common agitational program of organizing *bandhs,* public meetings, rallies and even pamphleteering among the general public.

According to the KNA, the Kuki tribes of Karbi Anglong district settled in their presently inhabited areas since the beginning of the early 19th century. It is a historically proven fact that in the process of their migration from the south towards the north, the Kuki tribes had happened to settle in the Mikir Hills and North Cachar Hill region. The Kuki tribes of the then Mikir Hills had settled in those part of the hilly terrain that was formerly in the Golaghat Sub-division of the then Sibsagar district of Assam. But these settled areas have now become part of the present Karbi Anglong district (erstwhile Mikir Hills). It is a well-known fact that the Kukis were freedom loving people and always find interior and isolated hilly region irresistible for their traditional *jhum* cultivation and enjoys freedom from other tribes and plains people. So, when they landed up in Mikir Hills, they instantly settled down in the hilly terrain which they found the region very much suitable for their free traditional lifestyle and *jhum* cultivation as the region was then a thick, interior and inaccessible jungle uninhabited by other tribes. Even today most of the Kuki inhabited areas are still found to be in deep interior places devoid of transportation, communication, and development.

Table 7.1: Tribe-wise Population of N.C. Hills (presently Dima Hasao) in 1854 and 1859

Tribes	*Mills' Report(1854)*	*Allen's Report(1859)*
Hill Cacharis	3,940	6,735
Hozai Cacharis	1,170	3,260
Mikirs	1,820	5,076
Old Kookies	3,335	3,709
New Kookies	7,575	4,763
Aroong Nagas	3,505	5,885

Source: Alexander Mackenzie

In 1946, when Mr. Murry the then Sub-Divisional Officer of Golaghat district visited the hilly areas he named it 'Kuki-Pahar' as it was predominantly inhabited by the Kukis. During the period beginning from the first half of the 19th century till 1926, no other hill tribes dared to settle in that part of the region primarily due to its inaccessibility which is utterly devoid of transport and communications with frequent occurrences of deadly diseases and natural calamities. But the Kuki tribes permanently settled down against enormous hardship and deprivation. Slowly and gradually the Kuki tribes could somehow bring the areas into habitable condition. From the latter part of the twentieth century, particularly due to population pressure on land and politics of the ruling powers to bring the region under their control, inflows of other tribes started in and around the Kuki-settled areas. Contrary to the earlier notion of the region being considered as 'no man's land', it started attracting the business community and profit-minded younger generation as they were enticed by the Kuki farmers making good profits from ginger, maize, arum and other agricultural products with the heavy annual turnout. In this connection, it may be noted that the Kukipahar (Singhason Pahar) is indeed famous for its bumper super-quality ginger production.

Causes of the Movement

Initially, the relationship between the Kukis and the Karbis were very cordial and they assisted each other in times of needs and difficulties. Even today the Kuki elders do narrates some of the past memorable incidents that took place in their relationship with the Karbis. In the past, the two communities had lived together with mutual trust and understanding. But with the passage of time, changes swept over the region particularly with the introduction of the new administrative set up under the Sixth Schedule. So, with the first general election of the District Council held in 1952, the politics of division and bargaining started in the tribal politics which is common in a democratic electioneering system.

The simple, shy and straightforward tribals very soon learned the game of democracy wherein majority rules and minority subdued. The political consciousness of the tribal leadership developed parochial attitude lacking consideration for others brought about the negative impact on the once cordial inter-ethnic relationship of various tribes living in the district. So, the new administrative set-up albeit significantly proved to be a great blessing for the major Karbi tribe, for other docile minor tribes of the district it is considered more a curse than a blessing as they could no longer voice and enjoy their rights and liberties as was in the past. District Council has therefore virtually become an instrument by which other minor ethnic groups and the Kukis, in particular, were by design prevented from having a place and space in the new administrative setup. The woes of the Kukis tribe ceremonially started right from the time when the District Council was instrumental for domination and exploitation by the major tribe. The KNA therefore strongly alleged that the Kukis inhabited areas were deviously dissected when delimitations of constituencies were carried out. They argued that this is deliberately done in order that the Kukis are deprived of a constituency in the district. The Kuki inhabited areas were truncated into pieces and merged with other neighboring constituencies depriving the Kuki tribes of having a constituency of their own. For the Kukis, the history of Autonomous Council is the history of their suffering and deprivation. Right from the beginning the Kukis having no representative in the Autonomous Council were constantly neglected and deprived of enjoying developmental benefits and activities conducive to their welfare and socio-economic development. The deliberate deprivation drives were meted out to such an extent that land disputes and other inhuman and mischievous acts have become the common order of the day. It is universally known fact that the tribal means of livelihood is agriculture. They entirely depend on the traditional mode of cultivation called *jhuming*. In this context, it is astonishing to learn that the Council supposed to be the protector and defender of the rights of the indigenous tribals has least regard and respect for the sentiments of the latter. The very question of their livelihood was under threat when the Council proposed to convert three fourth of the Kuki inhabited areas as Forest Reserve by the name 'Khonbamon' way back in 1975. It was, however, difficult for the Kukis to understand when a few of the Karbi villages located in the same areas were excluded from the purview of the proposed Forest Reserve and thereby exhibiting the venom of discrimination against the Kukis that compelled the Kuki leaders to approach the Honourable Gauhati High Court for justice.

The KNA alleged that the Kukis having no say in any administrative matters concerning themselves and their permanently inhabited areas, their lands were encroached upon by the Karbis that often ensued in barbaric and tragic killings like the one that took place in April 1990, wherein seven members of the Kuki community were slain. The manner in which the innocents were killed was horrific and merciless as they were put to slow death by cutting their throats with bamboo blades whilst tying their hands on their back. The KNA is also of the opinion that such kind of ghastly killing should have provoked hue and cry and protest of condemnation from all sensible citizens. But unfortunately, that did not take place. Neither a voice of condemnation nor any finger was raised against those perpetrators. This kind of incidents actually aggravated the situation that fast corrodes the age-old mutual trust and inter-ethnic relationship. The Kukis having lost faith in the ruling majority virtually developed a feeling of great insecurity and apprehension that their interest and welfare will never take care of under the prevailing circumstances wherein there are a strong tendency and attitude of exclusion and disowning politics of the ruling majority towards the minorities. They have therefore developed a feeling of fear and trepidation concerning their future in which they anticipated that they will never enjoy equal rights and opportunities with the majority Karbis, at least, under the existing political arrangement.

Table 7.2 Various ethnic tribal inhabitants of Dima Hasao and Karbi Anglong.

District	*Ethnic Tribal Inhabitants*
Dima Hasao	1. Dimasa 2. Jeme-Naga 3. Hmar 4. Kukis 5. Biate 6. Hrangkhol 7. Khelma 8. Jaintia 9. Karbi 10. Vaiphei
Karbi Anglong	1. Karbis 2. Bodos 3. Kukis 4. Dimasas 5. Hmars 6. Garos 7. Rengma Naga 8. Tiwas 9. Man(Tai Speaking)

Source: National Informatics Centre, Dima Hasao and Karbi Anglong.

Interestingly, besides the Kukis, other tribes of Karbi Anglong has also made a similar allegation that their names were deleted from the electoral roll that deprived them of their political rights to exercise their adult franchise in the elections to the Autonomous District Council, State Legislature, and Parliament. The KNA strongly resented that some irresponsible groups all along have been advocating that the 'Kukis are foreigners'. This kind of propagation against any indigenous groups in any part of the country is undemocratic and unethical and is against the very ethos of the Indian Constitution. Under such circumstances, the Kukis have no choice but to find ways and means for their future under the provisions and political framework of the Constitution. The KNA lamented that though the Kukis were great warrior tribes and have greatly contributed to the Indian freedom struggle for independence fighting the British Empire particularly in the historic Anglo-Kuki War of 1917-1919(Kuki War of Independence), the prevailing circumstances compelled them to develop the feeling that they were neglected and unattended under the new political regime after independence. The KNA in its series of memoranda had, therefore, highlighted the ruthless plight of the Kukis and how they were being demoralized, subjugated, neglected and exploited with a stepmother treatment in all dealings.

The Kukis clamouring for their own Autonomous Regional Council is mainly attributable to callous politics of parochialism, discrimination, nepotism and ethnocentric political game plan for narrow political gains. With such narrow political outlook, brute forces were also largely instrumental in enforcing the whims and notions of the domineering majority virtually disregarding the interest and welfare of the minority tribes. Certain leaders of the district also made it no secret of their discriminatory stance and intention to wipe out the distinct language, culture, and tradition of the Kuki tribes. Consequently, a wave of indignation swept over the minds of the Kukis of the district who saw the solution of their problems only in the creation of a separate Autonomous Region Council. So, the Kuki Chiefs and leaders from a different part of the district and neighbouring areas met together and following the thorough discussion on issues concerning their future unanimously resolved to formally organize themselves under the name and banner of KNA and with immediate effect launched their demand for creation of Autonomous Region with Autonomous Regional Council. Thus, the KNA was born to spearhead the movement for KTARC.

The KNA spearheading the movement represented about 35 thousand soul of the Kuki tribes inhabiting Karbi Anglong and has submitted a series of memoranda to different levels of authorities at regular intervals highlighting negligence and discriminatory treatment meted out to them by the Karbi Anglong Autonomous District Council in matters primarily of culture, development and atrocities committed by members of the Kuki tribes by the Karbis. The KNA is convinced that the permanent solution to the problems of the Kukis of Karbi Anglong is only in the granting of autonomy to the Kukis. They believed that nothing less than granting of autonomy will be able to bring them freedom from their present hardships and difficulties.

It is worthwhile to note that KNA is also one of the active sister organizations of the Citizens' Right Protection Committee (CRPC), an organization of all non-Karbi minor ethnic tribes of Karbi Anglong district. The main plank of the CRPC is 'negligence of the non-Karbis in Karbi Anglong district'. Similar to that of CRPC, the primary object of KNA is the well-being and advancement of the Kuki tribes and the establishment of the KTARC under the Sixth Schedule of the Constitution of India within the autonomous district of Karbi Anglong by peaceful and constitutional means. In pursuance of the objectives set forth, the KNA demand for creation of the Kuki Tribes Autonomous Regional Council within the Autonomous District of Karbi Anglong in accordance with the Constitutional provisions vide Sub-paragraph 2 of paragraph 1 of the Sixth Schedule of the Constitution of India. The proposed demand of the KNA for the creation of KTARC is to be established on the pattern of the Pawi Lakher Autonomous Regional Council. It may be stated here that Pawi Lakher Regional Council was trifurcated in 1972 to form Pawi, Lakher, and Chakma Regional Councils. The KNA articulated in their memoranda a list of their grievances that they felt can be rectified and the interests of the Kukis can be protected only if an Autonomous Kuki District(AKD) comprising part of Diphu Sub-division, Howraghat Sub-division, and Bokajan Sub-division is formed. The KNA had, therefore, submitted various memoranda to the Centre, State and District authorities demanding the creation of the proposed separate autonomous Kuki district. The KNA also made it clear that for any reason, if its demand for separate Autonomous Kuki District is not endorsed, it avowed its determination to fulfill and settle its aspiration for an Autonomous Regional Council as envisaged in the Sixth Schedule to the Constitution of India. The legal status of this demand is found in paragraph 1(2) of the Sixth Schedule (Autonomous Regional Council) and paragraph 1(1) (Autonomous District). With the subsequent stepping down of the KNA from its original demand of a full-fledged Autonomous District to an Autonomous Regional Council, it is even more firmed on its stance to achieve and accept nothing less than Autonomous Regional Council.

Table 7.3 Karbi Anglong District sub-Divisions.

Name of Sub-Division
Diphu (Sadar Sub-Division, H.Q.-Diphu)
Bokajan (Civil Sub-Division, H.Q.-Bokajan)
Hamren (Civil Sub-Division, H.Q.-Hamren)

Source: NIC, Diphu, Karbi Anglong.

Proposed Boundary of KTARC

The proposed jurisdiction of the Kuki Tribes Autonomous Regional Council shall be that of the following.

East: Begins from Saijang village in the South and running straight towards the North ending at the boundary of East Rengma *Mauza.*

West: Starting from the Saijang Kuki village in the East and running straight to the West up to any point on Patradisa River. This straight line will be running parallel to the National Highway (N.H.) 36.

South: From the point where the proposed boundary of the South on the Patradisa river and running straight towards East ending at Saijang Kuki village which is the limit of Southern boundary and the beginning of proposed Eastern boundary of the Region.

North: Up to the point where the proposed Western boundary begins on the Southern boundary of West Rengma *Mauza*, Naga Rengma *Mauza* and up to the point where the Eastern boundary ends at the Southern boundary of East Rengma *Mauza*. The area of the proposed Kuki Tribes Region will be in between 1500 sq. km. and 2000 sq. km. All the Kuki villages in that area fall within the proposed boundary of the region.

The Justification for Demanding KTARC

The Kukis of Karbi Anglong justified their demand for creation of the KTARC under the Sixth Schedule to the Constitution of India by reiterating their grievances, subjection, and helplessness under the existing Autonomous District Council of Karbi Anglong. They lamented that during the long period of its existence, Karbi Anglong Autonomous Council have not done any justice to the Kuki tribes living in the district in all respect concerning development and other promotional activities. Therefore, the Kukis could not get their genuine and proportionate share due to them at par with the Karbis and other tribals living in the district obviously because of their continued victimization through various calculated and vicious designs. The continuous neglect and discriminatory attitude of the leaders of Karbi Anglong Autonomous Council disappointed the Kukis and made them feel that they have no hope but a miserable and gloomy future ahead. Right from the beginning, a step-motherly treatment was meted out to the Kukis by the Council on all fronts with contempt and disregard of their sentiments and emotions. All these ruthless deprivation, neglect and continuous discrimination compelled the Kukis to explore all possibilities and find a solution to their long-standing problems that finally gave birth to KNA with a political aspiration to create the Kuki Tribes Autonomous Regional Council within Karbi Anglong district. According to the KNA, nothing less than the creation of Autonomous Regional Council for the Kukis under paragraph 1(2) of the Sixth Schedule to the Constitution of India will bring an end to their problems. The Kukis were utterly frustrated in the style and fashion Karbi Anglong Autonomous Council is functioning particularly towards the indigenous minority. Thus, hoping against hope, the Kukis have great expectations in the fulfillment of their demand in which they will then be able to manage their own affairs and preserve their social, cultural and political identity with the establishment of the Kuki Tribes Autonomous Regional Council (KTARC).

Response from the State Government

For realization and fulfillment of their political aspirations, the Kukis consistently struggled for the creation of Autonomous Regional Council since 1992. Henceforth, the KNA has been submitting memoranda and also held several discussions with the Government of Assam at various levels including the Three Members Ministerial Committee Constituted by the then Chief Minister of Assam, Shri. Prafulla Kumar Mahanta. The Three Members Ministerial Committee had initiated the process for the collection of views and comments from different parties including the Karbi Anglong Autonomous Council over the feasibility or otherwise for the creation of the proposed demand of Autonomous Regional Council by the Kukis. The KNA alleged that the Government of Assam and the Karbi Anglong Autonomous Council, in particular, has tactically delayed the progress of materializing its demand. The reluctant Autonomous Council endeavours to delay and even derail the process of preliminary groundwork initiated by the State Government. The Government of Assam has actually started expediting the initial process by directing the Commissioner of Hills and Barak Valley Division to submit a report on the demands of the KNA and their grievances thereof. Accordingly, Dr. D. Das, IAS, Commissioner of Hills and Barak Valley Division, Assam, Dispur had submitted his report on the 8th May 1995.

The report unambiguously stated about the grievances, neglect and atrocities committed against the Kuki communities along with other information and facts, such as, for the period of the Kuki settlement in Karbi Anglong for more than 150 years, their past relationship with the Karbis and the causes of conflict and tension between the two communities including the pitiably low level of developmental activities in the Kuki-dominated areas, size of their population, non-representation of the Kukis in the Karbi Anglong Autonomous Council and some major causes that led to the demand for an Autonomous Kuki Regional Council. Similarly, in pursuance of the Government Order, the D.C. of the Karbi Anglong district has also submitted his report to the Government of Assam on 18th June 1996, a year after the Government of Assam constituted a 'One Man Commission of Inquiry' (8th June 1994). Undoubtedly the Report was in favor of the demand of the KNA. Para 4 of the Report of the D.C. of Karbi Anglong is herein reproduced as below.

'In Karbi Anglong district the powers of the Karbi Anglong Autonomous Council has been enhanced with the entrustment of 30 more Government Departments. So far as decentralization of powers of Karbi Anglong Autonomous Council to the village level is concerned, it is found that no village council has yet been formed by the Karbi Anglong Autonomous Council and hence, there is a concentration of power at the level of Council in the district. The Karbi Anglong Autonomous Council is naturally under the domination of the Karbi people and there is widespread dissatisfaction that the benefits of the developmental programmes have not percolated down to Kuki villages and Kuki villages have remained totally neglected. Further, there are frequent complaints from Kuki National Assembly that Kuki tribes feel neglected and isolated.

Under such circumstances, taking into consideration their separate ethnic identity, a separate language, and custom, their feeling of isolation and suppression, it will be justifiable for the Government to consider their demand for creation of a Kuki Tribes Autonomous Region and Kuki Tribes Autonomous Regional Council within Karbi Anglong Autonomous district.'

The Government of Assam also directed the Karbi Anglong Autonomous Council to furnish its comment on the demand of the KNA for creation of Kuki Tribes Autonomous Region and Kuki Tribes Autonomous Regional Council within Karbi Anglong district for the first time in July 28, 1996 and with subsequent reminders on the 13th August 1996, 16th November 1996, 18th January 1997 and on 1st February 1997. The Karbi Anglong Autonomous Council pay no heeds to those reminders. However, the Karbi Anglong Autonomous Council informed the Government on 20.01.1997 that it would furnish its views at a later date. In response, the Government communicated the Autonomous Council to furnish the same positively by 10th February 1997. But till February 1997, the Autonomous Council of Karbi Anglong has not responded to the Government and thereby once again exposed its prejudiced and intolerant attitude towards other minority tribes with a clear intention to overlook the issue preferring to keep it in a continuous suspension. However when the demand has been asserted more vociferously and increasingly gained more grounds with supports from various organizations of other ethnic communities strongly favoring the legitimate demand of the KNA for creation of KTARC under the constitutional provisions of sub-para (2) of para (1) of Sixth Schedule to the Constitution of India, and pressure from the Government of Assam, the Karbi Anglong Autonomous Council eventually submitted its report. The Report of the Karbi Anglong Autonomous Council, however, did not favour granting of the Kuki Tribes Autonomous Regional Council within Karbi Anglong district; on the ground that, the granting of a Regional Autonomous Council to the Kuki Tribes would lead to the bifurcation of the existing Karbi Anglong district. But the KNA vehemently refuted the Report of the Karbi Anglong Autonomous Council and submitted a memorandum to the then Union Home Minister of India, Shri. Indrajit Gupta, on the 12th June 1997; wherein it categorically stated that in no way the creation of KTARC would lead to the bifurcation of the existing administrative and geographical boundary of the Karbi Anglong district. The argument put forward against the formation of Kuki Tribes Autonomous Regional Council, as communicated to the State Government by the Karbi Anglong Autonomous Council is baseless and therefore do not stand the test of reality. Contrary to the trepidation shown by the Karbis, the KNA firmly holds the view that the formation of KTARC will effectively improve the overall scenario of Karbi Anglong district wherein ushering peace, progress, and prosperity in all fields, and will be in no way detrimental to the growth and development of Karbi Anglong.

With the exception of Karbi Anglong Autonomous Council, the demand of the Kukis for Autonomous Regional Council within the geographical boundary of Karbi Anglong district had received warm approval from other non-Karbi communities of the district. The then Government of Assam was also in principle agreed to the legitimate demand of the KNA for granting autonomy to the Kukis of Karbi Anglong for which it has initiated the initial groundwork thereof.

The KNA demand for KTARC entered another significant phase when a Memorandum of Understanding (MoU) was reached between the KNA and the Holiram Terang led fraction of the ASDC on December 4, 2000, wherein the latter promised to the former to facilitate the creation of a separate autonomous council for the Kukis. This agreement is significant because the ASDC being essentially a Karbi dominated political party and the creation of KTARC was refused by the Karbi Anglong Autonomous Council, where the Karbis are in the center stage of powers. Later, this ASDC-KUKI MoU was made a big political issue. The Karbi militant group Karbi Longri Dima Hasao Liberation Front (KLNLF) launched an open campaign against the MoU alongside the rival faction of ASDC (Jayanta Rongpi group) raked up the issue creating political furor and confusion in the district risking yet another round of ethnic clashes between the Kukis and the Karbis that once took place during 2003-2004.

Kuki–Karbi Conflict and the Demand for KTARC

The greatest setback to the demand for KTARC was the outbreak of the Kuki-Karbi ethnic clashes in 2003. According to the KNA, it was a part of the undeclared and hidden agenda of the Karbi militant groups and terms it as 'ethnic cleansing'. The fact was established when a Karbi militant group in November 2004, has publicly come out for the first time against the demand of the KNA and the MoU signed between the KNA and the ASDC in 2000. This seriously retarded the growing demand of the Kukis for autonomy. Some immediate causes of the infamous conflict were brutal harassment committed on the Kuki villagers by the United People's Democratic Solidarity (UPDS) militants in conjunction with intimidation and extortion. The UPDS had also imposed an economic blockade on the Kukis and were also banned from their age-old practice of ginger, maize and other cultivation which were the only means of their subsistence and livelihood. But the Kukis of the district with 90.00 percent of them solely dependent on *jhum* could not subscribe to such diktat which is a blatant violation of their basic human rights; that too, from a militant group. The Kukis therefore strongly resisted and refused to comply with such order that forbidden them from enjoying their basic right to freedom to live and profession. The consequence of such reaction resulted in the costly ethnic clashed between the Kukis and the Karbis that lasted for about six months where both the parties suffered heavy losses. The root cause of the conflict happened to be the Kukis' demand for Regional Council. As the demand for autonomous regional council started gaining ground with all other non - Karbi communities fully supporting the demand, and in principle, the State Government favoring granting autonomy to the ethnic group have started preliminary works of collecting views and comments for the purpose, the Karbis in general and the Karbi militants, in particular, have become more apprehensive and thus declared war against the Kukis. The apprehensions of the Karbis have grown stronger as they knew well that the demand is legitimate and they cannot hold back in the long run. The KNA's demand is legitimate and justifiable in as much as the demand of the Karbis/ASDC for the creation of Autonomous State under the provisions of the Constitution. It is pertinent to note that, right from the time when the idea of Autonomous District Council was conceived, Regional Councils were strongly favored for people of distinct tribes having a distinct language, custom, and culture within Autonomous Councils. In fact, the Bordoloi Committee strongly recommended the establishment of Regional Councils if there are distinct sub-tribes within the autonomous district. The Karbis have no justification for opposing the KNA's demand for Regional Council, because if the demand for Autonomous State is just, rightful and constitutional, so also is the demand of the Kukis and vice versa. These weak points made the Karbis resort to the aid of the militant group that declared war against the Kukis which the KNA perhaps rightly termed it as 'ethnic cleansing'.

The Present State of the Demand

The ethnic conflict that took place between the two communities has virtually put the demand of the KNA in a state of suspended animation at present. For fear of another round of senseless ethnic violence and misunderstanding, the demand for regional council could not again immediately pick up its earlier enthusiasm of the pre-ethnic conflict period but hitherto remained in a dormant state with the office of the KNA now transferred on to the shoulders and responsibility of new leaders of the younger generation. So in the aftermath of the ethnic violence, the pace of the demand for KTARC has slowed down and virtually halted and could not yet fully regain its original spirit and strength to resume the struggle.

Conclusion

Increasing demands for separate statehood, homelands

and autonomy by different ethnic groups in the Northeast and Assam in particular, such as the demand coming from the Boros, the Karbis, the Dimasas etc. and the rising ethnic conflicts in the region is a harsh reality that calls for careful attention and proper handling of the situations. In Northeast, the tribulations need to look at from the perspective of ethnic consciousness and thereby our constitutional mechanism meant for such purposes need to be availed and applied wherever possible to absorb conflicting forces to uphold unity through sustaining diversity. In view of the increasing incidents of ethnic violence and threat coming from silent invaders from neighbouring Bangladesh, granting of functional autonomy to the Kukis would harm nothing but rather would improve and encourage the ethnic relationship, socioeconomic conditions of the people and political development, growth and stability in the region at large. It is, therefore, the responsibility of the government and the people concerned to recognize and consider the genuine demand of the Kuki community. I think it is necessary to address, redress and accommodate, if any section, community, region or even a hamlet of our body politic feels neglected or discriminated. This is exactly for which the provisions of the Sixth Scheduled to the Constitution of India is meant for. So, concerning the Kukis and their demand for Regional Council, it may be just apt to conclude with the opinion and submission made by the then D.C. of Karbi Anglong in his report submitted to the State Government on the issue; '.... *taking into consideration their separate ethnic identity, separate language and custom, their feeling of isolation and suppression, it will be justifiable for the Government to consider their demand for creation of a Kuki Tribes Autonomous Region and Kuki Tribes Autonomous Regional Council within Karbi Anglong Autonomous district.*'

References

1. Memoranda of the Kuki National Assembly.
2. Memorandum of the Citizens' Right Protection Committee.

3. The Assam Tribune, Dated, May 23, 1997
4. Northeast Sentinel, Dated, May 22, 1997.
5. The Northeast Times, Dated, May 24, 1997
6. The Assam Tribune, Dated, May 23, 1997
7. The Purbanchal Prahari, Dated, July 29, 1997.
8. The Assam Tribune, Dated, July 20, 1997
9. The Northeast Frontier Magazine, Guwahati, February 2004, p.37.

Chapter - 8

Socio-religious Movement and its Effect on the Rabhas of Assam

Surajit Kumar Pal

Religion is an integral part of every human society which is manifested and embedded in their belief system. The belief system is closely linked with spirituality (religious thoughts and beliefs), sanctity (holy/sacredness) and devotion (the activity of religious worship), where nature gets special weight-age from cognitive sense. Nature is equated with God and spirituality which are interwoven in character. Thus every human community, particularly the communities who are backward in terms of spiritual, cultural and socioeconomic progress, is the major concern in the present context. Their subsistence economy is simple and eco-oriented. They are often in the midst of nature's lap and for this reason, their survival is largely governed by nature. In other sense, historically they are considered to be at the bottom of civilization ladder and are remain isolated from the pace of human progress. This is applicable more in primitive[1] as well as relatively developed societies (as they are often connoted as tribal communities and hereafter 'tribal communities') whose techno-economic life is not at par with the advanced societies.

With the process of technological advancement particularly since the beginning of 20th century the tribal societies including the relatively developed societies, could not remain static and isolated completely from the advanced societies. The pace of adopting various technological devices, inputs and cultural aspects including religious observances and practices from the advanced communities started fast, especially after the Second World War. This has been possible with the extension of spatial communication network and other infrastructural development (construction of roads, establishment of schools and other academic institutions, extension of railway connectivity, telecommunications, establishment of rural markets etc) in most inaccessible areas where habitations of majority tribal and other marginalised communities (also known as backward communities) are located. In the present context, religion gets priority concern in this chapter. So the discussion on other aspects may have passive importance.

It may be mentioned that religion plays a significant role in moulding human mind to follow certain observances and rituals solemnized under religious norms and codes. Religious norms and codes are reflected among the members of any society in their religious behaviour which is embedded gradually in their social system. Moreover, religious norms and codes are closely linked with one's ethical principle. That means religion and ethics are also quite inter-related and inseparable from the cognitive system. Hence spirituality, sacredness or holiness, and devotion which later came into force in human societies with a continuous process of advancement of civilization over centuries are considered to be the basic components of religion.

Prior to such development human societies when they were in the phase of the pre-agricultural stage, used to worship various natural objects such as sun, stars, mountains, river, sea, tree, animal etc as gods and goddesses. Symbolizing these natural objects as gods and goddesses deeply rooted in man's belief system. This was a significant development in the context of human evolution, particularly the emergence of belief system in human societies. In other words, this belief system may be considered as one of the evolutionary developments in human societies that transformed gradually into religious behaviour embedded in human mind through different time scale of civilization.

In fact, religion is a common aspect of every culture world over. It is essentially subjective in nature. But the people belonging to either simple or complex culture express their religious belief through rites and rituals, ceremonies and festivals, symbols and songs etc. More specifically, the people of simple society often use natural objects as symbols. Therefore, symbolism ascribed to natural objects as gods and goddesses is more reflective of the belief system of simple societies. Worship of natural objects is a common practice among the people of tribal communities. They are considered as simple folk and their technology is not at par with the people of complex societies whose mental development as well as a belief system is very sophisticated and finer. So, the belief system is closely interlinked with supernatural power that cannot be ignored by any society – whether the people of simple culture or the people of complex culture.

Since the beginning of human civilization, man has been experiencing various odds of his life for existence on this earth. And in course of time, the belief system has been transformed towards the process of worshipping various gods and goddess who are believed to be the extra supernatural beings. These supernatural beings are worshipped by the gods and goddesses. The name of them varies from society to society of which some are benevolent and some are malevolent. Benevolent and malevolent impacts of deities mainly depend on its harmful and non-harmful effects among the people of the society. Livelihoods and survival of the simple societies are more eco-based than the people of complex societies and their belief system is nature based. They are usually called as animists i.e. the worshippers of natural things. However, to the members of any society – simple or complex form religion is always regarded as sacred or holy. The term 'holy' needs not be thought of as 'supernatural', much less as 'personal'. The terms like sacredness, devotion, pollution, and purity are value loaded. These terms, evolved later, prevail in almost all human societies. But its manifestation differs from society to society.

From the evolutionary point of view, it requires material advancement, mental sophistication, and professional expertise to develop finer specimens of symbols of God. Several centuries of trial and error went into the development of finer specimens. Human civilization has passed through the stages of natural worship, tool worship, fertility cult worship, theriomorphic worship and now anthropomorphic worship. To come to the case of some groups the people of simple culture, a long process of positive acculturation has put them in an advantageous position to quickly move to anthropomorphic image worship. This is now applicable to almost all human societies of the world including the tribal and other simple societies of cultures.

In the Indian context, the tribal communities[1] including the primitive and vulnerable tribes[2], are now under development paradigm for their socio-economic upliftment. For speedy and rapid development various development programmes are being executed in inaccessible areas where the people of various tribal communities live. Amongst them, the Rabha is one of the plains tribes of Assam distributed in different districts of the Brahmaputra Valley. They are mainly confined to Goalpara, Kokrajhar, Darrang, Kamrup and Dhuburi[3] districts of lower Assam. Their traditional belief system has been transformed greatly due to prolonged contact with the greater Hindu society. They have now become the anthropomorphic image-worshippers. They have passed through the process of various socio-religious movements started over a century back that helped them to be recognized as the Hindus. Being recognized as the Hindu certain traditional religious practices are equally important in their belief system which is still followed by them.

Traditional Belief and Inclination Towards Hinduism

Traditionally, the Rabha are the animists, worship

inanimate and natural objects like the sun, moon, mountain, hill, river, stream, trees, stone slabs, etc. In other words, they are the nature worshippers. However, they are, by tradition regarded as the 'natural Hindu'. Because it is associated with certain criteria for which the Rabha and other Indian tribes are treated as the natural Hindu. The criteria are: (1) accustomed to nature worship, (2) absence of any prophet, (3) spontaneous response to natural problems and prospects, (4) absence of holy-scripture, (5) absence of anthropomorphism, (6) presence of polytheism, etc. These criteria resemble the Hindu practices. Therefore, their way of life is based on the Hindu tradition. Apart from this, their territorial location was never secluded from the greater Hindu society for centuries. Rather, they are quite encysted by the Hindu communities.

In a traditional belief system, they attribute soul to the above-mentioned inanimate and natural objects. Like the Hindu, they worship various deities namely *Rishi*, *Rantak* or *Runtak*, *Baikho-Bai* or *Khokshi-Bai*, *Bai-Ma-bai*, etc. Amongst all these deities *Rishi* is the most important and supreme God, considered as the creator of the universe and lives in heaven with his wife *Jaga*. Both of them are identified as Lord *Shiva* and *Parbati* respectively in the Hindu pantheon, worshipped on community basis during the summer season under the shade of a particular tree or a hill. Their worship pattern bears certain similarity with the worship of the Hindus. They attribute the soul to him on a stone slab along with an iron trident symbolized as Lord *Shiva*, worshipped for the well-being of the whole community.

Rantak or *Runtak* is also identified as *Lakshmi*, the Goddess of Wealth as believed by the Hindus. Both are also considered as their family deities. To symbolize them every Rabha family in one corner of their living room keeps two earthen pots of unequal size with full of rice placed on a bamboo platform. The *trisul* (trident) is placed in between these two pots and the frontal view of the pots is marked with vermilion. Being the agricultural community, keeping them inside the room is indispensable for their sustenance, well-being as well.

A week-long harvest festival, known as *Baikho* or *Khokshi utsab* used to be celebrated on the occasion of Goddess *Baikho* or *Khokshi* puja, with great pomp and gaiety once a year during *Asar-Shraban* (May-June). The festival used to be organized at the *Baikhotoli* or *Khokshitoli*, located mainly in Bamundanga and Joyramkuchi villages of Mechpara area of Goalpara district. Joyramkuchi used to be familiar as Khokshibari to the local people of the area. Later, duration of this festival was reduced to three days only due to economic hardship and other reasons. In such festival young boys and girls used to take part in dance that continued throughout the night. Several healthy and fat yielded pigs are sacrificed to the deity for bumper crops, copious rains, and better health and free from natural calamities such as earthquakes, floods, and droughts, etc. During the festival days, they arrange grand feast substantiated with excessive consumption of *choko* or *chakot* (rice-beer). In other sense, it is symbolized as fertility cult as the marriageable boys and girls choose their life partners and later they used to be united by the nuptial bond. It bears certain significance that once they used to exchange their sweetheart in such festival, under no circumstance this could not be altered or violated by anyone of them. Now, this festival has almost disappeared from their society due to socio-political and other reasons.

Despite their tribal background they always claim themselves as the Hindus. Since centuries back they are within the milieu of the Hindu society. As a result, their interactions with neighbouring Hindu community on different affairs are deep-rooted and various socio-cultural traits of the Hindus have got the prominence in their social system. In the Brahmaputra Valley, Hinduisation process started in the medieval period particularly during the time of the great Vaishnava Saint of Assam – Sri Shankar Dev (1449 – 1569 AD) who propagated Vaishnavaism (a sect of Hinduism) among the Assamese masses including various tribal communities. He founded the Satra culture in the whole of Assam and his tenets greatly influenced the masses. The Assamese masses were given *saran* (spiritual initiation) so that the people could follow the path of Vaishnavism. During such period a large number of Rabha and other tribal population were greatly influenced by it and became the *Sarania*[4] (disciples or devotees of Sri Shankar Dev). After embracing this sect of Hinduism they modified their age-old traits and practices of nature worship and assimilated completely with the greater Assamese caste/Hindu society[5]. During such period process of the Bhakti movement founded by Sri Chaitanya Dev (1486 – 1533 AD) of Bengal was also simultaneously influencing various tribal and caste groups of Assam. Both these Satra and Bhakti movements were sustained for a long time. This has had certain historical significance in analyzing the process of socio-religious awakening taken place among different ethnic groups.

Although a sizeable Rabha population became *Sarania*, its larger masses remained as Rabha, but not isolated from the influences of Vaishnavism, founded by Sri Shankar Dev. And in course of time, they started to reform their age-old social system through which they could move towards Hinduism. With the reform movement, they were ultimately in the midst of the Hinduisation process. So, this was the beginning of their social awakening and enlightenment towards empowerment in religious and other spheres. And this phase can also be regarded as the first Renaissance period among the Rabha that enabled them to be claimed as a Hindu community. However, in this phase, they did not give up the practice of nature worship as asserted by them. They claim and also believe, nature worship is an integral part of Hinduism and interwoven in the sociocultural system of every Hindu group or community.

Claiming to be the Hindu they started to reform their traditional socio-religious practices, customary norms and rituals that enabled them to be the part of the Hindu society. However, worship of some old deities still gets importance in their socio-religious and belief system. Thus, worship of both traditional and Hindu deities is in existence in their socio-cultural system and various Hindu religious traits have been imbibed in their cognitive system. In a later phase, particularly during the early part of the 20th century, they entered the era of the second renaissance that touched the base of the whole Rabha society. During this phase, they consciously and voluntarily went deep to make further modifications in the socio-religious system.

The Era of Second Renaissance and Hinduisation

This era is very important that the Rabha society was moulded to take up several steps for social changes. They are: (a) spread of literacy from grassroots level, (b) unification of various Rabha sections by forming students' organisation, (c) propaganda against various social evils and superstitions, (d) codification of traditional norms and customs by publishing '*pandulipi*' [6], (e) formation of the Rabha National Council (RNC), the apex social organisation, (f) aspiration for political activities, (g) embracing Hinduism, Brahmoism, etc. This phase is often considered as the era of the second renaissance as the whole Rabha society aspired for social, cultural and political change.

The era of the second renaissance started mainly in the early part of 20th century. During this phase, the whole of the Rabha society was internally shaken and the members of its youth generation were enlightened in social, cultural, political and spiritual spheres to some extent. This was because some primary schools were set up in some pockets of their territory through which light of empowerment started among the young generation. At the same time, the waves of various religious forces were penetrated in their area and a sizeable population of different sections was influenced and spiritual enlightenment began among the Rabha masses. This was one of the landmark developments in the Rabha society. During such period of Hinduism, Brahmoism came into force from time to time particularly from the early decades of the

20th century that continued till the 1980s. This long span of time is considered as the most effective phase in the arena of cultural and spiritual transformation among the Rabha masses.

It is relevant to note that prior to 1916, the Rabha had no formal apex body to govern their society. They were regulated mainly by the village councils, headed by the headmen, popularly called the *Tangams* or *Madals* (or *Gaonburas*). Till the period of 19th century, no unity prevailed among different sections or sub-groups living in different places of the Brahmaputra Valley. During this century the area was quite isolated from road and other communication facilities and difficult to access. Even the area was surrounded by the dense forest where wild denizens were abundantly available. This situation compelled them to remain secluded from outside contact. Moreover, they were almost illiterate and their outlook centered on their villages itself that continued till the first decade of 20thcentury (Sarkar, 1976). Inaccessibility and their seclusion from outside world started to disappear when there was some improvement in the infrastructural facilities like road communication and the opening of some primary schools in certain pockets of their territory. This began to usher a new era in the Rabha society (Sarkar, 1976).

In this context, it is also mentioned that the youths who were empowered to some extent by pursuing formal education mainly at the level of the primary stage, felt the importance of unity of all sections for making the path of progress in different spheres. To fulfill this aspiration they wanted to have a platform for collective action through which poverty and socioeconomic backwardness could be eradicated from their society. But, their purposes were often thwarted by the elders who were so powerful in traditional village councils that the youths could not do much headway in achieving their goal. In fact, the traditional village councils functioned as a regulatory body as far as social control of the villages is concerned. The village councils used to be operative mainly in localized level, but not in the greater level. This hindered the unity move of different sub-groups into a strong, powerful and progressive community. This situation continued for several years in the first quarter of 20th century.

During that time the traditional village councils never thought the unity of all the Rabha sections. Rather, the village councils were largely responsible for brewing disunity in society. Over the time, influences of the village headmen and village elders started to wane that brought disquieting affairs in society. At this juncture, a young leadership emerged which wanted to bring a new social order by replacing the age-old social norms and customs. The new young leadership realized the importance of education, which they thought, could accelerate the pace of change in society. They also felt, once the Rabha masses are empowered with modern education, they would feel the significance of unity of the Rabha and would be conscious about the modes of exploitation and deprivation resorted to them by the non-tribal neighbours. During this phase, they used to often come in confrontation with the village elders on the issue of leadership and disarray condition in society. To overcome this situation the young leaders with progressive outlook came forward to form one platform for greater Rabha unity and safeguarding the interests of the Rabha masses. But their initial efforts did not much success due to various reasons (Sarkar, 1976).

The early decades of the 20th century are very significant in terms of the emergence of various socio-religious movements[7]. These have had a positive role in reforming their society to great extent. Of all religious forces, Hinduism was in the forefront which influenced the larger Rabha masses. The religious forces were responsible for hammering the base of their society that led to bringing a new set of norms and customs which were gradually accommodated in their social system. And at the same time a kind of social awakening also began to start among the youths of the Rabha society (Chakravarti, 1966; Sarkar, 1976; Sarkar, 1982; Pam, 1986; Pam, 1986). During this time social reform movements also started to bring dynamism in their society.

With the process of social reform, they had given up various age-old socio-cultural norms and customs which were considered major impediment of their socioeconomic upliftment that led them to remain backward in all respects for centuries. The reform movements spearheaded by the youths during those days played a significant role in cleansing various social evils and practices from their social system that generated conflicts between the youths and the elders of that time. This conflicting situation had also shaken the very base of their society. In spite of this situation, the youths were somehow able to take over the helm of their society and since that time the nucleus of political aspiration started to brew in the minds of the students and the youths' generation who were, in fact, the torchbearers of their society. In this regard, Gobardhan Sarkar (Rabha) was instrumental to motivate the students' community whose contributions were immense[8] in forming various social organisations[9].

Processes of social awakening and the Hinduisation were simultaneously operative as well as more effective in the first half of the 20th century for which the whole Rabha masses were proceeding towards socioeconomic and religious change. In fact, traditionally they are animists by faith, but with Hinduisation they adopted gradually the Hindu pantheon of worship as their gods and goddesses. They are the Goddess *Durga, Kali, Vishnu, Radha, Krishna, Shiva, Lakshmi, Saraswati, Mansha* etc. These Hindu gods and goddesses become now the part and parcel of their religious system. Various observances like *Janmashtami, Ekadasi, Purnima, Sankranti, and Shivaratri* are celebrated by them. They also take part in two famous festivals of Assam like *Bhogali Bihu* (celebrated on *Makarsankranti,* the winter solstice) and *Rongali Bihu* (observed on Assamese New Year's Day i.e. in April). They have also been influenced by various Hindu preceptors from time to time.

It is observed that some particular places are earmarked for worshipping their traditional deities. In addition, they have set up the Hindu *mandir* (temple) separately in their villages.

For example, in Debitola, a village of Kokrajhar district, *Radhakrishna Mandir* has come up under the title of *Govindashram* in the recent past. In Joyramkuchi, a *Shiva-mandir* exists which was built a few decades back by some Ram Vilas, a Bihari man who came to this village as a businessman. He was religious-minded in nature. With his active initiative as well as with the support of some villagers of Joyramkuchi, a *Shiva* temple came into existence in the village. The temple was consecrated with the installation of *Shivalinga. Shivalinga* used to be worshipped every day by the villagers. In this regard, a non-Brahmin priest was appointed to perform daily worship. After a few years of its existence, a Vaishnavite follower was appointed to perform the priestly duties.

Apart from this, very recently the Rabha of Joyramkuchi and its adjoining villages have become Vaishnavites. The prior to late 1970s this was absent in such area. This same trend is also noticed in some villages of Mechpara and Dudhnoi areas. They prefer to identify themselves as Hindu. Thus in recent years process of Hinduisation is more intensive in different parts of the Rabha Hasong Autonomous Council (RHAC) area because unabated infiltration from neighbouring Bangladesh and frequent ethnic clashes are one of the major reasons of this development.

The *Gobindashram* of Debitola is functioning to satisfy the religious aspiration of the local Rabha people. The idols of *Radha-Krishna* are worshipped every day as their god and goddess by the followers of Hinduism or Vaishnavism. The devotees of Debitola and its neighbouring villages assemble in every evening in the temple and take part in *bhajan* (devotional songs). They mark *tilak* (a sectarian mark) painted on the forehead and nose by smearing a paste made from a special type of clay. Marking of *tilak* identifies them as the Vaishnavites. Within a couple of years, a substantial percentage of the village population of Parbatjowar area (Debitola, Baghpara, Salbari, Jongipara, Kazigaon, Tokragaon, Barshijhora, Hatibandha, etc.) have been inclined towards Vaishnavism. Even those are still animists by faith, gradually influenced by Vaishnavite faith. They believe, Vaishnavism is nothing but a sect of Hinduism.

Although they are animists by religion, they are, on principle, the Hindu by nature as reflected in their behavioural pattern. Since time immemorial they have been influenced by Hinduism as it is the religion of the majority of the people of the country. For this reason, they claim themselves as the Hindu and also officially recorded as the Hindu. Apart from this, the Rabha of Parbatjowar Tract have been come in contact with various Hindu and Vaishnavite saints, visited the said area from time to time. Their occasional visits were responsible for bringing them to enter into the Hindu fold.

The impact of Hinduism varies from section to section. Among all sections, the people of Pati section have been greatly influenced by Hinduism. Pam (1986) reports that Chotamatia and other adjoining villages inhabited mainly by the Pati section of Dudhnoi Police Station were very exposed to the waves of various religious movements. The major religious waves came in their villages are Brahma Dharma, Christianity, Sanatan Dharma, Satsanga. But all these religions did not influence them deeply. So far the records are concerned that the villages of Dudhnoi Police Station especially the area up to the western bank of the Dudhnoi river was exposed to Hinduism first and then followed by Christianity, Brahmo Dharma, Sanatan Dharma, Vaishnav dharma, and Satsanga. Barring Christianity, all other aforementioned religious sects are considered as facets of Hinduism. The village, Chotamatia played a significant role to lead a sizeable Rabha masses in the sphere of spiritual development as this village has been passed through successive religious waves.

Brahma Dharma, a religion founded by Raja Rammohan Roy, the first and foremost thinker of modern India, had the great vision of a united, free and theistic India. The Rabha, particularly the members of the Pati section were once deeply influenced by the Brahma Samaj of Calcutta. The name

Brahma Samaj is closely associated with the social history of modern India. The role of this Samaj was immense in the evolution of the Indian societies in both the19th and the first part of the 20th century. The motto of his religion was the spiritual worship of the one eternal God, the creator, and father of all.

The Brahma Samaj advocated a universal religion which knew no barriers of caste, colour, race or nationality but united men and women of all classes and countries (Sarkar 1982:2). In other words, Brahmoism is the religion of the future humanity born of the union of the east and the west. He always pleaded to remove all sorts of inequalities embedded for centuries in different sections of the Indian society. The aborigines, depressed classes were most subjugated by the forward and advance section of the society. This hurt the souls of the great thinker as well as his ardent disciples. To remove various social disabilities like untouchability, backwardness, illiteracy etc., the Sadharan Brahma Samaj (SBS) started a cell in the name of 'Depressed Classes and Untouchability' which operated in the backward sections like the Scheduled Castes and tribes spread in the states of Assam, Bengal, Bihar, Orissa, etc.

Among the tribes, the Khasi, Garo and the Rabha Missions were functioned of which the Khasi Mission is the oldest. The Garo and Rabha Missions were mainly confined to Goalpara district of Assam. The Rabha Mission of the Brahma Samaj worked in Goalpara from 1927 and it continued till the 1950s (Chakravarti and Ray, 1996:65). The most peak period of the said Mission continued in between the 1930s and 1940s.

The spread of Brahma religion among the Rabha of the south bank of the Brahmaputra River (Goalpara district) started with the initiative of Dwarikanath Rabha of Shantipur who made contact with the Bramha Samaj in 1926 for the opening of the Bramha Mission among the Rabha people. This religion was confined mainly to the Pati section of the Dudhnoi Police Station area. Of course, some members of the Rongdani section of the Goalpara Police Station came in contact with the preachers of Brahma religion. But their number was negligible. This religion was spread in Damra, Darranggiri, Rangjuli, Salpara, Chotamatia, Barmatia and other villages of the Dudhnoi Police Station. All these villages are inhabited mainly by the Pati Rabha. Abinash Chandra Lahiri, one of the ordained missionaries of Brahma religion was deputed to the tribal areas of the Brahmaputra Valley from the Sadharan Brahma Samaj, Calcutta for preaching this faith among the tribal people. The main motto was to bring the tribal people under the fold of Brahma religion.

Hence, Abinash Chandra Lahari's name is closely associated with the Rabha Mission of the Brahmo Samaj. He traveled extensively in the Brahmaputra Valley and was involved in preaching the Brahma religion among the Rabha and the Garo. He used to visit both the Rabha and the Garo villages off and on and extended spiritual discourses to these people. The prominent Rabha and Garo Brahma followers of those days are Rajendra Narayan Rabha, Chandrakanta Rabha, Pahu Ram Rabha of Darranggiri, Kalta Ram Rabha, and Baikuntha Behari Rabha of Chotamatia who led to bring the Rabha masses of south Goalpara under Brahma religion. To cater to the spiritual needs of the Brahma followers the Brahmo *mandirs* (temple or congregation hall) were also set up in the villages mentioned above. Of all these villages, Darranggiri, Salpara, and Chotamatia were leading in social, cultural and religious activities.

The followers of this faith used to assemble for prayer in the Brahma temple on various occasions like *Maghotsab* (a religious festival observed by the Brahma followers in the month of *Magha*), *Bhadraotsab* (a religious festival celebrated in the month of *Bhadra*), *Nababarsha Utsav* (celebration of Bengali New Year), foundation day anniversary of the Brahma temple, rites the passage etc. During these occasions, all the Brahma followers used to take part in prayer, Brahma *sangkirtan or bhajan* (recitation of devotional songs), *Brahma Sangeet* (singing of devotional songs related to Brahma religion) which were followed by community feast. The expenditures for these rituals were borne by the followers of this faith. Marriage, birth and death rituals used to be performed according to the edicts and rules of the Brahma religion.

It reveals from the records of the Sadharan Brahma Samaj that the followers of Brahma faith spread in different villages used to meet in the *Brahma sanmilans* (conferences) organized usually in Chotomatia, Salpara and Darranggiri villages. In such conference, various concerned issues like social, economic, healthcare and educational problems were to be discussed. In these conferences, Abinash Chandra Lahiri, the then in-charge of the Rabha Mission used to come and presided over the function. The other prominent Brahma representatives like Principal Satish Chandra Roy of Guwahati, Shibanath Dutta of Shillong were to be present in such congregations who used to be invited from Guwahati and delivering talks on different issues like education, women's empowerment, tenets of Brahma religion, social reform, economic problem, etc.

Besides annual ritual services and conferences, they used to celebrate the birth and death anniversaries of Raja Rammohan Roy, the founder of the Brahma Samaj and other prominent Brahma leaders like Shibanath Shastri, Kesab Chandra Sen, and others. In 1941 when Gurudev Rabindranath Tagore expired at the age of 80 years, a special condolence prayer service was organized in all Brahma Samaj Mandirs of the Rabha areas as a mark of respect to the departed soul of Gurudev Rabindranath Tagore.

In this context, it may be mentioned that the expenditures incurred for the Brahma sanmilans, annual conferences, a celebration of *Bhadrotshab, Maghotsab, and Nababarsha Utsab* (New Year's Day) and other occasions were to be met from the collective fund created in every Brahma Samaj Mandir. The followers of the Brahma families used to contribute cash or kind (mainly paddy) to each Brahma

Mandir fund formed for the purpose of organizing various aforementioned Brahma functions as well as for running various welfare services like homoeopathic dispensaries, night school, free library, etc. The sale proceeds of paddy were regarded as the main source of income for each Brahma Mandir. There was also a separate fund other than the general fund raised in every Bramha Samaj Mandir for the welfare of the Rabha women.

Contributions and Impact of Brahma Dharma

Faith in Brahma Dharma has had positive contributions in the sphere of spiritual, cultural and socio-economic development of the Rabha society. Its proper evaluation is yet to be done that may have certain impacts on the evolution of the present-day Rabha community. Spreading of Brahma religion among the Rabha was not only meant for religious enlightenment but had also the purpose of bringing social change in this tribal community as reflected in objectives of the Rabha Mission. It is reflected in its welfare activities done in different Rabha villages of Dudhnoi Police Station for improving their socio-economic backwardness.

The welfare activities started with the establishment of free homoeopathic dispensaries functioning in Darranggiri and Chotamatia that continued for several years. Expenses for medicines were to be borne by the authorities of the Sadharan Brahma Samaj, Calcutta. Apart from this, in September 1941 one Brahma primary school was also established in Baramatia for propagating literacy among the Rabha, Garo and other local downtrodden masses. In the beginning, the school was co-educational, started with twelve students of both sexes. Along with the primary school, the one-night school was also functioning for the illiterate elders, involved mainly in agricultural activities and labour works. During the agricultural season, the school remained closed for facilitating the elders to take part in agricultural works. But after some years functioning of both the schools was closed permanently due to lack of patronage of the Sadharan Brahma Samaj and local support and response.

In order to women's empowerment in the sphere of education, healthcare, economic pursuits, etc., 'Brahma Mahila Samiti' (Women's society) was established in every Bramha dominated village. Moreover, a library was set up in Chotamatia for promoting literacy and reading habits among the Brahmas and non-Brahmas. The books were to be distributed of this library to the villagers of Salpara, Baramatia, and other adjoining villages.

In addition to the Brahma Mahila Samiti, the grain reservoirs were set up on a cooperative basis in every Brahma Samaj Mandir to create food security for the cause of the needy Brahma followers during the lean period when they faced economic constraints to sustaining their families. Indeed, these cooperative grain reservoirs played a great role in saving them from the exploitation of the unscrupulous money-lenders.

Apart from grain reservoirs, both women and youth wings were formed in every Brahma Samaj of the village for their spiritual and moral development and also for motivating them in pursuing some gainful economic activities for improving their socio-economic backwardness. With this motto, the authorities of the Sadharan Brahma Samaj tried to extend all possible help in establishing weaving centers on a cooperative basis in Chotamatia and other Brahma influenced villages for augmenting their family income. Every year youth and women conventions were to be held to discuss various problems responsible for the impediment of the overall progress of the Rabha society.

The impact of Brahma religion on the Pati Rabha section of Goalpara district is immense that cannot be ignored. During those days when they were social, economically, educationally, spiritually and politically were much backward, this religious faith influenced and enlightened them to adopt broader outlook towards their people and society. Today the people of the said area are ahead in education, political leadership, and other spheres compared to other sections. Chotamatia has produced some illustrious Rabha personalities whose leadership in social, cultural and political fields is immense and significant in the realm of their upward mobility. Notwithstanding that the activities of the Revolutionary Communist Party of India (RCPI) led by Soumendranath Tagore, a descendant of Rabindranath Tagore's family of Calcutta in Rabha area started mainly from Chotamatia, Salpara and other adjoining villages of Goalpara district. It also influenced a sizeable Rabha masses empowered politically to great extent. Indeed, the RCPI gained ground in the Rabha area where the spread of Brahma religion had taken place. S.N. Tagore, also the follower of Brahma religion got the privilege to do his party activities among the Rabha that lasted for several years. Undoubtedly the members of the Pati section were forefront in political awareness amongst the whole Rabha masses and in this regard contributions of the RCPI leadership are noteworthy that could never be blurred or overlooked. In other sense, the RCPI was perhaps the pioneer in sowing the seeds of left ideologies among the Rabha masses.

However, their social, political and spiritual awakening got some set back when the waves of Brahma religion started to wane due to the demise of the prominent Brahma followers of Chotamatia, Salpara, Baramatia, Darrangiri, Damra and other villages of Goalpara district. With their demise, the patronage of the Sadharan Brahma Samaj, the apex institution of Brahma religion was to be ceased for obvious reasons. But its impact among the Rabha still remains unevaluated due to lack of adequate primary and secondary source of information. In spite of this lacuna influences of this religion undoubtedly enlightened them to adopt a new outlook on their society and culture which embedded gradually in their cognitive level. That's why this faith continued to influence them for long years.

The Rabha society has influenced by the impact of another Hindu religious sect, the Satsanga, founded by Sri Anukul

Thakur[10] (1888 – 1969). *Satyanusaran* (the pursuit of truth) is the main pillar of his faith. It has occupied a special space on their spiritual level. In the mid-1960s some prominent Rabha persons of Chotamatia and other villages of Dudhnoi Police Station and Salpara, Barjuli, Baida and other adjoining villages of Mechpara Estate area were the pioneers to adopt such religion. In subsequent years its number has increased considerably. Now a sizeable Rabha population are its followers, distributed in different parts of the RHAC area. And they are spiritually identified themselves as the '*Satsangis*'. After becoming the satsangis they prefer to have vegetarian food; because of features/edicts of *Satsanga* stress on vegetarian food as it keeps mind fresh and pure maintains good health and good character. Its impact is not mass-based, rather, limited to a sizeable Rabha population only.

It is evidenced by empirical findings that after taking *Diksha* (initiation) from the Satsanga preachers the Rabha belonging to the Pati, Rongdani, and Maitori sections are identified internally as the *'Satsangi'*. But it does not bear their community identity as 'Rabha'. Unlike the Sarania they have never given up their tribal identity which is indispensable to their survival and entity. So, as a tribal community, it is also important to enjoy the constitutional privileges for socioeconomic advancement. Despite inclination towards Hinduism, they are always conscious to project their own tribal identity

In recent time, conversion to an alien faith is a sensitive issue in India. Despite this, in the recent past, a sizeable population of one section (the Koch) of the Rabha has been converted to Christianity. But they are not the pioneer to accept this alien faith. Prior to them, a few Rabha persons of South Goalpara have converted to Christianity of which Rev. Jahaj Rabha of Miapara village was perhaps the first Christian among the Rabha of Assam (Rabha, 1987:43). Later Hariprasanna Rabha of Amguripara and Haliram Rabha of Barpathar of South Goalpara were some notable Christians.

Authentic documents or history about Christianity among the Rabha are not readily available even today.

In pre-independence period some attempts were made to take evangelical activities among this indigenous group. But that venture of the Christian missionaries was not much successful among the Rongdani, Maitori and Pati sections due to the stiff opposition from the then Rabha leaders who were quite against of conversion to an alien faith. Later, various Rabha organizations also adopted some positive steps to counter the activities of Christian missionaries. Instead, they played a significant role in embracing Hinduism by amending their customary norms and rules. As a result, the Rabha in general despite sectional variation were stuck to their own faith which still prevails in their cognitive level. Thus, proselytizing activities for conversion among this community was negligible.

However, in the post-independence era, some Catholic and Baptist missionaries had a dent to make the venture in conversion works among the Rabha of some villages of Goalpara and Kokrajhar districts. The Catholic missionaries concentrated their works mainly among the Rongdani and Pati sections of Goalpara district, while the Baptists were involved among the Koch (also called as the Kocha) section of Parbatjowar area of the then Dhubri district (now Kokrajhar district). The Catholic Christians are negligible in number scattered in Darka, Chechapani, Toplakhowa, Barabakra and Damra villages of Goalpara district. The churches of these villages are governed by the Tura Diocese of Meghalaya and parish services are also accorded by this Diocese (Panachickal, 1996).

On the contrary, conversion to Christianity among the Kocha section in the Parbatjowar Tract and other parts of Kokrajhar district has spread rapidly as reflected in the establishment year of the churches made between the late 1960s and the early 1980s (Table 8.1). It reveals from data, embracing Christianity among the Kocha section started first over half a century ago in Kalbhandari village of Parbatjowar Tract. In his writing, Rabha (1984:1) reports that in Kalbhandari village about 30 families embraced Christianity. But under certain circumstances and under stiff opposition and social boycott resorted to them by the opponents of Christianity they were compelled to revert to their old faith after a few years. However, amongst them, the two converts were stuck to this faith despite facing various odds and miseries. And these two persons were the pioneer to light the message of Jesus Christ in the Kocha villages.

Table 8.1 List of Churches affiliated to the RBCU, Assam

Sl. No.	*Name of the Church*	*State*	*Year of establishment*	*No.of families*	*No. of persons*
1.	Kalbhandari	Assam	1969	38	180
2.	Dolmaka	‘	1969	19	125
3.	Ambari	‘	1970	18	94
4.	Hatibandha	‘	1983	40	179
5.	Debitola	‘	1976	36	186
6.	Salbari	‘	1976	35	172
7.	Sapkata	‘	1960	31	145
8.	Amlaiguri	‘	1970	36	219
9.	Ghaksha	‘	1971	40	283
10.	Rampur	‘	1972	14	70
11.	Islampur	‘	1972	28	107
12.	Moynaguri	‘	1978	29	122
13.	Gaonsulka	‘	1978	28	179
14.	Jaleswari	‘	1980	3	16
15.	Charaidaka	‘	1975	9	33
16.	Sindhrijhora	‘	1980	8	41
17.	Chechapani	‘	1980	8	41
18.	Magurmari	‘	1980	4	32
19.	Charaigaon	‘	1979	5	26
20.	Panbari	‘	1983	8	40

Source: Rabha Baptist Church Union (RBCU), Debitola, Dhubri District, Assam.

In 1957 Rev. Rex Glasby, an Australian Baptist missionary came to Debitola, a backward village of the Dhubri subdivision of undivided Goalpara district inhabited by the Kocha section for evangelical works. At the beginning of this initiative, a dispensary was first established in Debitola for extending health care facilities to the local people. At the same time, the foundation of the Rabha Baptist Church Union (RBCU) also started for missionary activities. He and his wife stayed for some years in Debitola and rendered valuable services to the new converts. Under his leadership, the mission activities started from Debitola in 1959. During his tenure, some Rabha villages of Parbatjowar Tract were brought into the fold of Christianity. After him, another Australian Baptist missionary Rev. Neville Kirkwood headed the RBCU till 1969 and in the same year, the leadership of the RBCU was finally transferred to an Indian pastor, Rev. Rokhama of the Zoram Baptist Church Union (ZBCU) of Mizoram. And its management still rests in the hands of the ZBCU.

Now the RBCU has rooted firmly in Debitola with different activities by running of Sunday school, dispensary, one primary school and an English medium secondary school and by spreading the evangelical message to the masses. In both, the school's local children belonging to the tribal and non-tribal communities are admitted and have got an opportunity to receive a quality education.

Impact of Christianity

Conversion to this faith leads to bring some significant socio-cultural changes in individual and community life. Their adherence to this faith has brought an undercurrent tension and conflict in society. Sometimes both converts and non-converts are at loggerheads on the issue of conversion. It is reported that in the initial phase of conversion frequent tension between the converts and non-converts used to be observed. But in course of time, this has been subsided to great extent. Despite conflict and tension, no serious violent incidents have been reported so far on the issue of Conversion.

Because their kinship bonds are so rigid that could never occur any violent incident in society. Hence a harmony between them still prevails in the concerned area.

Interestingly both converts and non-converts belonging to the same family can stay under one roof as noticed in Debitola and its neighbouring villages, but take a meal from the separate hearth. Even in the initial phase of conversion when they were less in number, marriage alliances often took place with the members of the non-converts, because non-availability of adequate marriage partners among the converts was acutely faced. This phase of adjustment continued for several years. Now a substantial number of marriage partners are available within the converts' families as a sizeable number of the Kocha families have opted for conversion to Christianity. Obviously, a phenomenal growth of Christian population has taken place. In fact, this development is one of the important changes found in this section.

After enrollment in Christian fold, they are abided by the Christian norms and ethos in respect of marriage, death and other life-cycle rituals. The Church is the main religious institution which plays a vital role in moulding one's socio-cultural and religious behaviour. Even in certain cases, it acts as a political institution as noticed in some Christian states of northeast India. Now the Christian Kocha members living in different villages have empowered to some extent in the sphere of education and politics and in this regard role of the Church is immense.

Moreover, the transformation is strikingly observed at different levels. They are: (a) given up their traditional ethos and norms in respect of religious belief and other practices, (b) economic upliftment by abandoning of some evil practices like drinking of *Choko* (rice-beer), smoking of *bidi* and cigarettes, etc. (c) attending church service on every Sunday, (d) consciousness in health care, (e) reviving and learning of traditional weaving by the womenfolk as existed in every family in the past, (f) compulsory sending the children to schools, (g) exploring opportunity for exposure to outer world, etc. For their economic upliftment, the RBCU authorities have adopted certain steps in the Debitola Mission compound of which weaving training center for women, a hostel for school children hailing from distant places, the introduction of scholarship for the needy and meritorious students are notable.

Christianity has also brought changes in the pattern of residence, inheritance, and succession. The Rabha was once a full-fledged matrilineal tribe. Now they have switched off from matrilineal to patrilineal system considerably. Shift from matrilineal to patrilineal principle is a major breakthrough in their society. For example, the newly married couples irrespective of their faith prefer to live either in neolocal or in patrilocal residence. In the case of inheritance, sons can inherit due to share equally with the daughters. Presently after the father's death office of the successor goes to the eldest son. As the successor of the property, he has to discharge the responsibilities of looking after the management of property and the family.

Despite conversion the followers of Christianity, who are negligible in number compared to the entire Rabha population, are not debarred from representation in various Rabha organizations like the All Rabha National Council (RNC), All Rabha Sahitya Sabha (ARSS), All Rabha Kristi Sangha (ARKS), All Rabha Students' Union (ARSU), etc. Although Christianity has brought some conflicts in their society, it could not affect the unity of all sections in the sphere of social, cultural, economic and political levels. Rather, the entire Rabha masses irrespective of sectional variation are always in favour of the unity of all sections to project a single community as well as to maintain their distinct 'Rabha' identity.

In this regard, the All Rabha Sahitya Sabha (ARSS) has conducted several language seminars in different places of the Rabha Hasong and outside the Hsong areas time to time for making the standard Rabha textbooks for the Rabha children. In such seminars, various common words used among the members of different sections were collected and standardized to use in writing the Rabha dictionary and school textbooks. The Govt. of Assam has introduced Rabha medium at the primary level in recent time. Altogether 78 Rabha medium schools have been opened in different parts of the Rabha area. This indicates how the Rabha as such are conscious of the unity of all sections for maintaining their own survival and entity.

Conclusion

The Rabha society has passed through various socio-religious movements spearheaded by different groups from time to time. Every movement has a certain positive direction towards social change. The Rabha, once a backward tribal community living in different parts of lower Assam, have been influenced by various religious forces since the 19th century. They have been transformed from animism to a full-fledged Hindu community by amending their customary norms and laws, though one of its sections (the Kocha) has embraced Christianity in recent years. In spite of their adherence to Christianity, it could not affect the unity of the whole Rabha society. Rather, the majority of the Rabha masses, by and large, profess Hinduism and claim themselves as the Hindu.

Crystallization of social awakening started in an early part of the 20th century through which various Rabha organizations came into existence. In such context, various socio-religious processes contributed largely to bring awareness among the youths about their society and culture. This awareness also stirred their mind to uplift socio-economic condition of the poverty-stricken Rabha masses and at the same time, they felt to maintain solidarity among different sections. But their feelings were not easy to implement due to various socio-political reasons. During that time inaccessibility to the Rabha area and conservativeness of the traditional leadership was the major impediments towards the unity of all the sections. This lacuna began to disappear when the youth leadership came to take over the helm of the affairs of the society. The new leadership first stressed on the spread of literacy, the formation of social organizations and adopting the policy of unity of all sections. These steps later have brought significant transformation in this society.

Meanwhile, with the process of social awakening waves of various socio-religious forces started to influence the people of different sections spread in different parts of the then Goalpara, Kamrup, Darrang and other districts of lower Assam. Of all religious forces, Hinduisation and Brahmaism were deeply responsible for moulding their mind for spiritual, social and political thinking. This transformation helped them later to take the task of social reform in society. The codification and publication of customary laws in the form of *pandulipi* are one of the important steps of social reform that bear significance in the sphere of maintaining social equilibrium and governance. In the present context, this step is also relevant to strengthen the unity of all the Rabha to a vibrant and progressive community.

In this regard one point is to make here that any kind of social and religious emancipation has taken place so far in the Rabha society, the agro-economic base is directly and indirectly associated with this development. The Rabha is basically an agrarian community and their economy is based on agriculture. Whatever the expenses made by the followers of Hinduism, Brahmaism, Satsanga or Christianity was borne from the sale proceeds of agricultural produce gathered from them. In other sense, economic support for celebrating any religious observances or festivals related to foretasted faiths is linked to the agrarian economy of the followers. Thus, their social system is quite integrated with the agrarian economy.

Their changes are found to exist in social, economic, political and religious spheres as reflected in the formation of the Rabha Hasong Autonomous Council (RHAC), All Rabha Sahitya Sabha (ARSS), All Rabha Students' Union (ARSU), political outfits like the Rabha People's Party (RPP), Rabha Hasong Demand Committee (RHDC), etc. The formation of the RHAC is a landmark development in the history of the Rabha society. It is approved by the government for safeguarding their identity and culture, resource management, retaining their demography from the onslaught of rampant illegal infiltration of the alien population of neighbouring Bangladesh. Now they are very conscious about the illegal migration that causes recent ethnic violence occurred in their territory on the issue of land and forest resource.

Under the recent volatile political situation in the Brahmaputra Valley, phenomenal change is noticed in their attitude towards the non-Rabha communities (Bodo-Kachari, Garo, Assamese, Bengalis, Muslims etc) living in the RHAC area. Changing scenario is also noticed in building the educational institutions, temples, Churches, etc. in different prominent Rabha localities. Organizing the 'Dadan Mela' and 'Baikho' festival is another dimension of their transformation. Occupational mobility and change of status are being emerged gradually in their society. Now they are competing with other advanced communities for seeking higher studies, jobs in public and private sectors. In fact, this kind of transformation among the Rabha bears special significance in the context of making their historiography. Undoubtedly effect of social awakening substantiated by various socio-religious movements has largely contributed this development emerged in the Rabha society and in future what new set of changes will emerge in their society that can only be ascertained and to is recorded by the future researchers.

Notes

1. According to the People of India Survey (1985 – 1992) undertaken by the Anthropological Survey of India altogether 4635 communities were identified, locate and studied throughout the country and out of which 461(9.95%) communities were identified as 'tribes'. But in recent time this number varies as some communities have been included in the tribal list of India due to

various socio-political and socio-religious movements emerged in different parts of India. Even some communities are waiting to be enlisted in the Scheduled Tribes' Order of Govt. of India (see the People of India, 'Preface and Introduction' of the National series, Vol.III – The Scheduled Tribes).

2. Govt. of India has listed 75 tribal communities separately as 'Primitive tribes' among the existing tribal list of India. They are defined as the primitive tribes, based on some major criteria. They are (1) pre-agricultural level of technology, (2) extremely low level of technology and (3) declining or stagnant population, (4) low level of literacy, and (5) economic backwardness. The above criteria were applicable mainly in 20th century particularly the period of its second quarter when their areas were devoid of basic infrastructural facilities namely roads, educational institutions, market centers etc for which they were remained isolated from the contact of the outer world. But in recent time this cannot be applicable as the inaccessible areas have now been connected with the market and urban centers. Now the primitive groups (PTGs) are moving gradually towards progress in different fields. In the Indian context, the aforementioned criteria are not applicable now except a few Negrito tribes of the Andaman Islands and some Mongoloid tribes of Arunachal Pradesh.
3. The Parbatjowar Tract of Dhuburi district has now been annexed to the Bodoland Territorial Autonomous Council (BTAC) area of Kokrajhar district where Rabha villages are located. In Dhubri district the Rabha are found to live in some villages only.
4. Persons who are the followers of Shri Sankardev, the great Vainavite Saint of Assam, are connoted as the Sarania.
5. It is historically proved that since medieval era the greater Assamese Hindu society as seen today was enriched largely by assimilation of different tribal communities of Assam namely Ahom, Bodo-Kachari, Rabha, Tiwa, Mishing etc.
6. Pandulipis means a codification of customary laws published by various Rabha Anchalik Committees like the Mechpara Madhyanchal Rabha Samaj, Dudhnoi Paschiomanchal Rabha Sanmilan, etc. The same also gets amendment time to time for governing their society.
7. Since the beginning of 20th century, the Rabha started to become enlightened spiritually and culturally when their society was influenced by the waves of various religious forces like Hinduism, Brahmoism, Satsanga and Christianity that continued till the 1980s. All the socio-religious forces were, directly and indirectly, responsible for bringing the social reform in their society that

has led to bringing a new set of norms and customs, embedded gradually in their social system. And with the process of various socio-religious movements social awakening also began to start among the youths of this society (See Gobardhan Chandra Sarkar, 1976: Background History of Origin of the Rabha National Council (RNC): Reminiscence (unpublished handwritten memoir in Assamese); Satis Chandra Chakravarti. 1966: Brahmo Samaj, Depressed Classes, and Untouchability (second edition). Calcutta: Sadharan Brahmo Samaj; Hem Chandra Sarkar. 1982: The Religion of the Brahmo Samaj, (3rd edition). Calcutta: Sadharan Brahmo Samaj; Rabin Pam, 1986: 'Atitar Jilingani' (in Assamese), in Jilingani, a souvenir of the Dirma Jamat Sanmilan, edited by Charu Mohan Rabha, pp.1-5. Chotamatia: Jilinguni Prakashan Samiti; Ganapati Pam, 1986: 'Dharmiya Sanskritir Prabhab' (in Assamese), in Jilingani, a souvenir of the Dirma Jamat Sanmilan, pp 43 – 50.

8. Gobardhan Chandra Sarkar (Rabha) was a prominent personality of Rabha society. He witnessed various phases of change in his society that has been recorded in his handwritten memoir (Sarkar, 1976 op.cit). In such memoir, he portrayed the activities of various Rabha organizations that contributed a lot in moulding the present shape of the Rabha National Council (RNC), the apex socio-political organization of the Rabha. He was instrumental to motivate his contemporaries and the students' community of that time for bringing social reform in Rabha society. With his active initiative, a movement for the unity of different Rabha sections was gradually crystallized in the then Goalpara district through which a self-determined and politically conscious Rabha society is seen today.
9. The evolution of the present-day All Rabha National Council (ARNC) or the Nikhil Rabha Jatiya Parishad (NRJP) took place in 1970 through various Rabha organizations functioned from time to time. They are the Assam Rabha Chhatra Sanmilan (1926), Assam Rabha Sanmilan (1926), Assam Rabha Yubak Sangha (1941), Assam Rabha Jatiya Seba Sangha (1948), All Assam Rabha Jatiya Sanmilan (1956), and All Assam Rabha Sangha (1963). After 1970, to strengthen its activities as well as for a wider unity of all the Rabha masses spread in Assam, Meghalaya, and West Bengal, its units have been set up in recent time. Now it functions as the apex body of the Rabha society.
10. Sri Anukul Chandra Chakravarty became familiar to his followers as 'Sri Anukul Thakur' or 'Sri Thakur', was born on 14 September 1888 in Himaitpur village of Pubna district of erstwhile East Bengal (now Bangladesh). He set up a Sansang Ashram for

fostering spiritual development, first at Pabna (now in Bangladesh) and then at Deoghar in India in 1946. The Satsang Ashram at Deoghar has now become a major place of attraction there. This sect of Hinduism is based on four ideals namely (a) education, (b) agriculture, (c) industry, and (d) good marriage. 'Satyanusaran' (the pursuit of truth) is the main pillar of this sect.

References

Chakravarti, Satis C. 1966. *Brahmo Samaj. Depressed Classes and Untouchability* (second edition). Calcutta: Sadharan Brahmo Samaj.

Pam, Ganapati 1986. 'Dharmiya sanskritir prabhab' (in Assamese), *Jilingani,* A Souvenir of the Dirma Jamat Sanmilan, pp 43 – 50.

Pam, Rabin 1986. 'Atitar Jilingani' (in Assamese), *Jilingani*, A Souvenir of the Dirma Jamat Sanmilan. Edited by Charu Mohan Rabha, pp.1-5.Chotamatia: Jilingani Prakashan Samiti.

Paul Panachickal, 1996. 'Impact of Christianity on the Rabha', In J. Puthenpurakal (Ed): *Impact of Christianity on Northeast India.*, pp. 322-328. Shillong: Vendrame Missiological Institute Publications.

Rabha, Mani 1987. 'Dharmiya sanskritir prabhab' (in Assamese), in *Silver Jubilee Souvenir of the Dudhnoi Paschimanchal Rabha Sanmilaan.* Edited by Ganapati Pam, pp. 42 – 44. Chotamatia: Dudhnoi Paschianchal Rabha Samaj.

Rabha, Prabhat Chandra 1984. 'Goalpara Rabha Baptist Unionor Chamu Itihas', (in Assamese), Brief history of the Goalpara Rabha Baptist Union, In *Silver Jubilee Souvenir of the Rabha Baptist Church Union* (RBCU), 1959 – 1984, pp. 1 – 6. Debitola, Dhuburi: Rabha Baptist Church Union.

Sarkar (Rabha), GC. 1976. '*Background history of the origin of the Rabha National Council (RNC): Reminiscence*'. Unpublished handwritten memoir (in Assamese).

Sarkar, Hem Chandra 1982. *The Religion of the Brahmo Samaj*, (3rd edition). Calcutta: Sadharan Brahmo Samaj.

CHAPTER - 9

NAMASUDRAS IN ASSAM

N.B. BISWAS AND N.R. ROY

Caste concept is a unique concept in the history of ethnographic study in the world in general. There is a racial division from the very evolution of man and society in the world. However, the caste concept is unique in the world literature, because of that no other country of the world is having such practices except Indian sub-continent. The populations are divided between India based on the caste. The classes are also determined in relation to the caste in these subcontinents. Although the people refer the Vedic literature so far, the caste is concerned; but during those time caste and class was determined based on vocation or profession not based on birth or any other component through the passage of exploitation of the elite and of the riches over the poor and the depressed. Although tremendous development and changes have taken place in India and the country has reached the age of science and technology and converted it into a knowledge society, but that knowledge society hardly helps to overcome the barrier or the discrimination of caste politics and caste-ridden societies. Hence, there is a need of in-depth study to examine the evolution of schedule caste and of with various groups and communities for breaking down this rigid caste barrier and bring them to the main society through the process of equality, equity, and humanity. The present chapter is an attempt to look into one of the segments of the schedule caste especially the Namasudra in Assam.

The Caste system has got it origin in the Indus Valley Civilizations and flourished as early as 2500 BC. The term 'caste' has been widely used to describe ranked groups within rigid systems of social stratification and especially those which constitute the society of Hindu in India. The debate over whether castes are found outside of India has intensified with increased knowledge and understanding of the Indian caste system. The term so used may be applied to such groups as 'Negroes' in South America and the 'Lowey-ETA' of Japan but only in India, there is a comprehensive caste system in which every member of the population is given a particular caste status. The basis of caste was set forth in the code of 'Manu' over two millennia ago. Many tribal and peasant groups came within the Hindu caste system. Many such groups were accorded very low social status and they were termed as untouchables and named as '*Panchama*.

History of India may be divided into four periods. First, The Vedic period ending about B.C 600 and comprising the literary data of the Vedic *Samhitas* and the Brahmans; second, The post-Vedic period, extending to about the third century of the Christian era. In this period, we have three types of literature, which shed light on this subject. The sacred laws of the Aryans present the Orthodox and the more or less idealistic standpoints while the epics testify to the contemporary practices. The third period may be styled the period of the *Dharma-sutras* and ends with the tenth or eleventh century A.D. Manu, Yajnavalkya and Vishnu are the chief exponents of the social ideals of this age. The fourth period may, with properly, be called the modern period, and it brings us down to the beginning of the nineteenth century. The customs and belief of contemporary Hindus are those that were mostly fixed and classified by the writers of this period. It was during this period that the present day vernaculars of India were being evolved. It must be mentioned in all the periods all the literary accounts of the important aspects of caste center around the four orders in society, namely Brahmin, Kshatriya, Vaishya and Shudra and the multifarious groups, which are the present-day caste.

In the Rig-Veda, the earliest work of the first period three classes of the society are very frequently mentioned and named Brahma, Kshatra, and Visha. The first two represented broadly the two professions of the poet-priest and the warrior chief. The third division was apparently a group comprising all the common people. It is only in one of the later hymns of the celebrated Purushasukta that a reference has been made to four orders of society as emanating from the sacrifice of the primeval Being. The names of those four orders are given there as Brahmana, Rajanya, Vaishya and Shudra, who are said to have come respectively from the mouth, the arms, the thighs and feet of the body of *Prajapati* lord of all creatures. The particular limbs associated with these divisions and the order in the society of the time, though no such interpretation is directly given in the hymn. This origin of the four classes is repeated in most of the later works with variations and interpretative additions. The Taittriya Samhita, for example, ascribes the origins of those four classes to the four limbs of the creator and adds an explanation. The Brahmins are declared chief because they were created from the mouth, punning on the word 'Mukha'. The Rajanya is vigorous because they were created from vigor. The Vaishya are meant to be eaten, referring to their liability to excessive taxation, because they were created from the stomach, the receptacle of food. The Shudra, because he was created from the feet, is to be the transporter of other and to subsist by the feet. In this particular account of the creator, not only is the origin of the classes interpreted theologically, but also a divine justification is sought to be given to their functions and status. The four classes are described as of divine origin, although in a later hymn, must be taken as a sufficient indication that they were of long duration and very well defined, even though the exact demarcation of their function, the regulations guiding their inter-relations, and the extent of their flexibility may not be referred to in the main body of the Rigveda literature, which avowedly of a liturgical nature.

These classes or orders are regularly referred to in the later literature as Varnas, so much so that popularly Hindu religion has come to be defined as Varnashrama Dharma. Yet in the Rig-Veda, the word 'Varna' is never applied to any one of these classes. It is only the Aryan Varna or the Aryan people that are contrasted with the Dasha Varna. The Shatapatha Brahmana, on the other hand, describes the four classes as the four Varnas. The colour connotation of the word was so strong that later on when the classes came to be regularly described as Varnas, four different colour was assigned to the four classes, by which their members were supposed to be distinguished.

The practice of casteism in the society was very much serious when the Aryan people came to India. Before the Aryan people, the Indus Valley Civilization prevailed in India. The Indus Valley Civilization is most probably a genuine gradual growth on Indian soil but an importation by immigrant foreigners establishing a colony in India. The sudden almost explosive rise of this Civilization and its spontaneous growth may have several causes. The great fertility of the soil caused the population to increase rapidly. Though initially, the population of the Indus Valley civilization may have been a uniform race, it did not remain so, for the skeletons found in the cemeteries of the sites show a mixed racial composition. Since the chronology has been revised and the end of the Civilization fixed at about 1750 BC, the old hypothesis has been revived that the Aryan invaders. The early forerunners of the Rig-Veda Aryans might have destroyed the centers of the Harrapan Civilization and killed or dispersed its population. Thus, the Aryan people dominated the native and they had spread their own culture, religion, social rules, regulation etc. it is worthwhile to mention that the so-called native people were known as Non-Aryan or Dravidian. The Dravidian or Non-Aryan people also had the rich culture and society but not as the Aryan. But the Aryan people came with very rich culture and knowledge; so they easily dominate the Non-Aryan people. The Aryan people started the process of Aryanization and the Non-Aryanization, and as a result, so-called Hinduism or Hindu culture came out. It has been mentioned earlier that in Rig-Veda the people of the society were divided into three groups viz. - Brahmin, Kshatriya and Vsha and the Shudra people came out as the result of Aryanization process. The process of Aryanization refers that those Non-Aryan people adopted all the rules, regulation and culture of Aryan by means of *'Suchi'* (purification) will be considered as 'Suchikrita Dravidian' or 'Shudra'. These Shudra people were considered as very lowest group people in the society. Because the Shudra class was largely formed by those aborigines who had accepted the overlordship of the Indo-Aryans and had entered into their service is more than probable.

Shudra and their Social Position

The 'Shudra' the fourth category of people of the society during the Vedic period were suffered a lot from various aspect of the society. They were considered as the lower group people because they are the Non-Aryan; just they have adopted Aryan culture and religion. They are considered as the lower because they have come from the feet of the Creator (God) mentioned in the hymn of Purushasukta. The Taittriya Samhita ascribes the origins of those four classes to the four limbs of the Creator. The Brahmins are declared to be the chief because they were created from the mouth, punning on the word 'Mukha' (mouth and chief). The Rajanyas are vigorous because they were created from vigour. The Vaishyas meant to be eaten, referring to their liability to excessive taxation because they were created from the Stomach, the receptacle of food. The Shudra because he was created from the feet. But in Bhagawat Gita Lord Krishna narrated the origin of caste system in different ways. Lord Krishna speaks to Arjuna (Bhagavad Gita Chapter-4, shloka 13).

caturvarnyam maya srstam gunakarmavibhagasah.
tasya kartaramapi mam viddhyakartaramavyayam..4/-13.

The fourfold order was created by Me according to the divisions of quality and work. Though I am its creator, know Me to be incapable of action or change.

Caturvanya; the fourfold order: the four varnas are named- Brahmin, Kshatriya, Vaishya, and Shudra. This constitutes the fourfold order. The three Gunas- Sattva, Rajas and Tamas- and the laws of karma- these four elements were divided by Me to create the four varnas.

The Shudras were treated very badly in that society so far as their social status is concerned. This class represented domestic servant, approximately very nearly to the position of slaves. The Shudra is described as 'the servant of another', 'to be expelled at will', and 'to be slain at will'. The Pancha-vimsha Brahmana defines this position still more precisely when it declares that the Shudra, even if he be prosperous, can't but be a servant of another, washing his superior's feet being his main business. Yet according to the same work, some of the king's ministers were Shudras. The milk to be used for fire obligation was not allowed to be milked by a Shudra. He is declared to be unfit for sacrifice was being offered. The Shattaptha Brahmana goes to the length of declaring that the Shudra is untruth itself. The illicit connection between an Aryan male and a Shudra female is mentioned, and uneasiness felt by the Shudra husband whose wife is a mistress of an Aryan is also hinted at. In this connection, we may mention that Vasishtha quotes a Brahmana text to the effect that a woman of the black race, meaning the Shudra people, was meant only for enjoyment and not for the furtherance of any higher motives.

Among the four Varnas, the old distinction of Aryan and Shudra appear predominantly as Dvija and Shudra, through the old distinction is occasionally mentioned. The first three Varnas are called *dvijas* (twice-born) because they have to go through initiation ceremony which is symbolic of rebirth. This privilege is denied to the Shudra who is therefore called 'ekajati' (once born). It is well known that in the story of Ramayana Rama is represented to have killed a Shudra who was practicing austerities. The Shudra was regarded to be so despicable, that a Brahmin when, out of sheer necessity, he had to make up the Shudra's occupation, was asked not to mix with them. So, it is clear that the Shudra could not perform a sacrifice, could not listen to or recite the Vedic text, nor could he practice austerities. He was categorically denied the right of initiation and consequently the first stage of individual life the studentship. Shudra had no right to perform any of the important sacraments. As he couldn't kindle the sacred fire, his marriage was certainly not regarded as a sacrament, intended for the fulfillment of religious duties but only as a sexual union.

The Mahabharat says that the Shudra can have no absolute property because his wealth can be appropriated by his master at will. If the master of a Shudra has fallen into distress, the latter shall be at the disposal of the poor master. The king is enjoyed to appoint only persons of the first three classes of villages and towns for their protections. Shudra trying to hear the Vedic texts shall have his ears filled with molten tin or lac; if he recites the Veda his tongue shall be cut off, and if he remembers it, he shall be disremembered. If he assumes a position of equality with twice-born men, either in a sitting, conversing, ongoing along with the road, he shall receive corporal punishment. A Shudra committing adultery with a woman of the first three castes shall suffer capital punishment, or shall be burnt alive tied up in straw. If he intentionally reviles twice-born men or criminal assaults on them, the limbs with which he offends shall be cut off. A Shudra committing adultery with an Aryan woman shall have his organ cut-off and his property confiscated. According to Kautilya, a Shudra calling himself a Brahmin shall have his eyes destroyed by poison or shall pay the heavy fine of eight hundred '*ponas*'. If he violates a Brahmin female he shall be burnt to death. If he intentionally reviles or criminally assaults a Brahmin the offending limbs shall be cut. Kautilya prescribes the differential rate of interest for debts according to caste, a Brahmin being charged 2.0 percent a Kshatriya 3.0 percent, a Vaishya 4.0 percent, and a Shudra 5.0 percent. It shows that how the Shudra was being treated in that contemporary society. Though they are very poor so far as their socioeconomic condition is concerned still they had to pay the highest interest. According to Dharmashastra, in the case of eating and drinking, if one had received food or beverage from a Shudra, he was ordered to do *prayasitta* by 'suppressing his breath seven times a day for seven days. Any Shudra male who had had sexual relations with a twice-born woman would be heavily punished by having his genitals severed and his wealth confiscated, and if the woman has a husband or patron of some kind, these aforementioned punishments will be followed by death.

Manu told that scholarship, education, acquisition, of knowledge except for one's own hereditary and traditional occupation, is sternly prohibited for the Shudras (Let not the Shudra be anywhere around where the Veda and other holy books are being taught or recited. This is an absolute prohibition if there be a Brahmin so foolish as to permit a Shudra to acquire knowledge; he is to be boycotted from religious functions).

Further, the Shudra can't be permitted to acquire or perform jobs, are meant only for the Brahmins and the Kshatriyas.

Therefore, from the above, it is found that the Shudra people suffered a lot for a long time. The Shudras had no place within the Aryan society. They had no any right even. They were servants to be disposed of at the master's whim.

The Schedule Caste

The scheduled castes are the people who belong to the last varna namely the Shudra or Avarna or Antyaja. The expression 'scheduled caste' was first used by the Simon Commission and embodied in the Government of India Act of 1935 in section 309. Before 1935 they were known as untouchable or exterior castes or depressed castes.

In 1901, Risley, the then Census Commissioner attempted for the first time to classify the Hindu castes but his classification was rather broad. He divided the entire community merely into seven categories. Then in 1911, an inquiry was held to ascertain which of the castes and tribes were discriminated against, on religious and social grounds. In 1921 this caste was mentioned as a depressed class for the first time. Now the question is who are the depressed or so-called untouchable?

Manu said to have mentioned the untouchables should be called Anya, Antyaja and the Antyavasin, and put their abode outside the village. The Antyajas were also Avarnas-those not belonging to any of the four Varnas or castes. So, the Shudra is a Savarna while the untouchable is an Avarna i.e. outside the Chaturvarnya or the system of four castes. According to Dr. Ambedkar, 'the word Antya in Manusmriti means not the end of creation but end of the village. So they were called Antyajas or Antyavasins. They would not live along with the Savarnas, not even with the Shudra, as they were the Atishudras.

According to the Hindu law codes, the Chandala, the representative of the Untouchables of ancient times, was the offspring of a Shudra father and a Brahmana mother i.e. the offspring of the most condemned Pratiloma marriage. Chandala came into existence in the dying stages of the later Vedic Era (1000-600 B.C). It is necessary to remember that earlier in the same work it is stated, almost in so many words, that the breed of Chandala is a degraded one and is ranked with that of the dog and pig.

The Dharmasutra writers declare the Chandalas to be the progeny of the most hated of the reverse order of mixed unions, that of a Brahmin female with a Shudra male.

Kautilya, the practical administrator who provides for a number of these so-called mixed castes, agrees with the Dharma- writers in the view that of the mixed castes those that arise out of the unions in the inverse order be spoken violation of Dharma, yet looks upon all of them as mixed castes. The treatment of Chandalas who, as we know, were an ethnic group already referred to in Vedic literature and one or two similar groups may further scan in order to shed light on the origin and the problem of the scheduled caste in general. There was a group separately recognized by Vasishtha, which was called Antyavasayin which he declared was the progeny of a Vaishya female by a Shudra male. In this way Svapaka came out from the progeny of Kshasttri male and an Ugra female said Manu, Mitrapas is another group which also came out in combination with Chandalas said Patanjali. Patanjali remarked that there were other groups than Chandalas and Mitrapas who had to live out the limits of Arya villages and town.

As it is mentioned earlier when the Aryan came to India, the process of Aryanization and Non-Aryanisation were started and as a result, Shudra, Chandala, Mitrapasa, Domb, Svapachas and other lower group peoples came out in the Indian society. It is worthwhile to mention that the Aryan people kept all these people under control and slowly and surely, these group people deteriorated in their social position between the time of Panini and that of Manu. In the former, as they lived within the limits of the village in which other order and castes lived. In the age of Manu (X, 51-2) they were not only excluded from the village but were assigned duties and prerequisites which clearly show that they were looked upon as vile specimens of humanity.

Namasudra is a sub-caste of scheduled caste, which was previously known as Chandala and recognized as the untouchable group in the society. Though they were considered as Chandala, their evolutionary aspect shows that they were neither Shudra nor Chandala rather they are the Brahmin offspring as their origin. Due to the unavailability of resources lot of misconception were prevailing in an earlier time and they were treated very badly. In the present chapter, that is why an effort has been made to clarify the misconception so far.

Thus, the present chapter entitled 'Namasudras in Assam' is designed with a view to examining their genesis, development and their position in the society, especially in Northeast India.

The Namasudra is a major caste found in Assam, West Bengal and another state of Northeast India. This group of peoples is recognized as the socio-economically backward and scheduled under scheduled caste category in our Indian Constitution. At the very ancient time, the Namasudra people were known as the Chandala is because their status was low on the social scale is considered to be a clean untouchable group. The different synonymous of the Namasudra are Chandala, Channel, Namasud, and Nama. In the Vedic literature so-called untouchable were known as Chandala. In the literature, it is found that Chandalas are the mixed caste. The references to the Chandalas in the Yajurveda clearly show them to be degraded people. In the next period, Chandalas are described as the offspring of a Shudra father and a Brahmin mother. They were considered as the degraded because they are the outcome of illicit unions between Aryan females and Shudra males.

In the Rig-Veda time, the Shudra people were considered as the lowest group in the society is because they are the fourth category people so far as the social structure is concerned at that time. The practice of Castism in the society was very much serious when the Aryan people came to India. They made classification of the society's people according to their work what they did during that time, but later on, this classification came into existence according to their heredity. They made the classification according to the quality of the people such as- Brahmin, Kshatriya, Vaishya and Shudra. Out of these categories, the Brahmins were considered as the superior in that period and the Shudras were considered as the lower. They were considered as the lower group people because they are the Non-Aryan; just they have adopted Aryan culture and religion. Again, they are considered as the lower as well as untouchable later, because they have come from the feet of the Creator (God) mentioned in the hymn of Purushasukta. The 'Shudra' the fourth category of people of the society during the Vedic period were suffered a lot from various aspect of the society. In the census of 1901, at which caste names and caste precedence were scrutinized and registered rather minutely, the Chandalas of Bengal, who was otherwise known as Namasudras. However, the Namasudra people were considered as Chandala in earlier text of India, but there is a controversy between the Namasudra and other people about their origin. Because it is only Ballal Sen then lord of Bengal considered the Namasudra people as Chandala and untouchable. Actually, the Namasudra people have their separate history of their own; they believed that they are neither Shudra nor Chandala; rather they are the offspring of Brahmin male and Shudra female.

Evolution of Namasudras

If we analyze different religious scripts and 'Jatitatta' books of India then we will find that the Namasudras are neither Chandala nor Shudra rather they are the Brahmin offspring. As we have to know that during the Aryan period due to the process of Aryanization and Non-Aryanisation Shudra people evolved. In another way, the Shudra people were considered very lower during that period as because they were born out from the feet of the Lord or Creator of all creatures. Chandala is who according to the scripture a progeny of illegitimate liaisons between Brahmin female and a Shudra male. During that period a higher caste people could marry a lower caste people and that was accepted in their society after purification, but the vice-versa could not accept and their offspring were referred as Chandala and they were considered as untouchable later. Therefore, we find that

Chandalas are the offspring of Shudra male and Brahmin female. However, the history of Namasudra is different; they are not offspring of Shudra male and Brahmin female rather they are the offspring of Brahmin male and Shudra female. Namasudras are not Shudra which has been narrated by so many writers such as- Shri Gourpriya Sarkar in his book 'Jatitattwa Sangraha' (Bengali), Shri Jitendra Nath Majumdar in his book 'Jatitattwa and Namasudra jatir Utpatti' (Bengali), Shri Jogredra Chandra Majumdar in his book ' Namasudra Jati Tattwa Katha' (Bengali), Shri Sattya Ranjan Sarkar in 'Namasudra Jatitatttwa' (Bengali), Shri Sukumar Sarkar in 'Namasudrai Parsav Bipra' (Bengali), Shri Darakanath Mandal in 'Namasudra Jatikatha' (Bengali), Dr A.K. Biswas in ' The Namasudras of Bengal' by referring different quotations from various religious books and by putting some example.

In the above-mentioned books the authors have placed that Namasudras are neither Shudra nor Chandala rather they are Brahmin offspring by birth, but because of some socially imposed force they lost their identity as Brahmin and as a result they had to live like a Shudra for their survival. The evolutionary history of Namasudra may be narrated in the following ways-

> The Namasudra is a very strong group in comparison to the other caste in Bengal. However, nowhere of the Indian scripts have mentioned the term Namasudra including Veda and other religious books in present society. Nevertheless, the question is why it happened and what the reason behind of this is. In the oldest religious book of Hindu just mentioned about four group of people such as- Brahmin, Kshatriya, Vaishya and Shudra but not about the Namasudra. Then what is the position of Namasudra and in which category they are belonging to? Or, how they have evolved in this world? After a long investigation one book named 'Shakti Sangam Tantra' (in Sanskrit) was found in Bengal and there the evolution of Namasudra

was narrated. In that book, there is chapter named 'Prantoshi' where Lord Shiva narrated the story about Namasudra to goddess Parvati in their conversation. In that book, it has been narrated that the great saint 'Namash' was the son of saint 'Kashyapa' whose father was lord 'Brahma's' son 'Marichi'. The wife of Saint Namash, Sulochana was pregnant when he left home for *tapsya* for a long time. When he returned home after 14 years then he found that his wife has given birth to two sons named 'Kirttiban' and 'Kuruban'. However, his wife Sulochana expired just after the sixth month of her delivery and two saints 'Afshar' and 'Naidhruba' looked them after. After his arrival, the saint 'Namash' was very much satisfied with his two sons and he wanted to make them purify by giving sacred thread as it is the ritual of Brahmin. But he couldn't make them purify as because they crossed their age limit 12 years. Then the saint 'Namash' again left home for a long time for his son's purification and up gradation in the society. After a long wait, Kirtiban and Kuruban left home for searching their father and finally they reached to a king named 'Simanta' in present Siliguri. The king Simanta was Shudra king and he had no son but, he had two daughters named 'Shipika' and 'Shapitraka'. Then the king made them agree to marry with his two daughters, and finally, they got married with those two girls thought they were Shudra by birth. In the course time, Kirtiban and Kuruban produced a number of children after their marriage, later on, these groups of people were known as Namasudra. The word 'Namasudra' had its two parts i.e. 'Namah' and 'Shudra'; these two parts have been borrowed from the memory of their forefather saint 'Namash' and mother (their mother was Shudra). Actually, the name of Namasudra was given by Lord 'Narayana'; when Saint Namash succeeded from his Tapasya then Lord Narayana gave him three boons, after getting satisfaction from his prayer. The three boons were - (i) that through your sons married with Shudra girls still, your generation will be equal to a Brahmin, (ii) that your generation will be known by your name i.e. they will be known as Namasudra and (iii) your name will be immortal. From that day onward the word Namasudra evolved and these group people also evolved.

The Namasudra people are of Brahmin origin which may be accepted from the cultural point of view also. In Manu's Doshakosh Pangika it is mentioned that-

Namasudra jatakhyata sampradaya samved adhikari!
Dashadishabadhya souchya palanang purusanakramena arjhyrate!
Tirthe pravashe grehavashe cha shraddha karjhya!
Tena pakkanna pindadang bidhi drishyte!!

It is also known from the 'Ballal Charit' that for the sake of a personal promise given to a Dom girl named Padmini to be married, the Bengal emperor Ballal Sen was obligated to invite the Kashypiya Brahmans to attend and participate in the midday meal party on the very day of engagement ceremony with the girl. But as a result of the refusal of the invitation, the armed forces of the king were directed to tear off the 'Holi Brahmin Thread' through force and dexterity. Accordingly, the Kashyapiya Brahmins of 'Mulghar were tortured highly physically as well as mentally. These deprived Brahmins were later on entitled as 'Namasudra' during the time and took the shelter in East, West, South and North Bengal and also in the place of Andaman Nicobar Islands from their Mulghar (presently Josohar in Bangladesh) residential area. During the period of 1158-1179 (Ballal Sen dynasty) the 'Namasudra' of Bengal were deprived and neglected in all terms due to the continuation of the ill effect of Sen time. During that period Ballal Sen conferred the name Chandala in place of Namasudra and he had abolished the name Namasudra from all kind of known religious book forcefully, and he made a rule that those who will not consider

Namasudra as Chandala they will be suspended from the job and they will be physically punished.

In this way, the other caste people considered Namasudra people as Chandala and they started to lose their power, fame, right, property, education etc. and in course of time, they were considered as untouchable like other Shudras in Bengal.

During the British period also Namasudra people were considered as Chandala or Charal; which the Namasudra people opposed and started agitation against so-called higher caste people. The year of 1872 was very important in India. Before 1872 some states and some districts were sending annual census statistics. The British Govt. however undertook first of All India Census in 1872. This Census recorded every caste and tribe of India. The govt. as a matter of policy went by the advice of the pundits regarding caste determination. It is worthwhile to mention that classification of castes and tribes by district magistrates were generally impartial, while the pundits and the native officials often failed to overcome caste prejudices and their enumeration cannot be considered objective. Sometimes they misled the census commissioner. It goes to the credit of the district magistrate, they on many occasions differed from the native census officers. Even British census executives were presumably influenced by the native officers. The striking indigenous Bangas (Namasudra) the most memories of people of East Bengal nerve accepted the slang 'Chandala' which the Aryan brought it from Aryandom and slapped on them. These tribes were formerly dominant and it only because they lost their political supremacy and have fallen under the Yoke of the Brahmanas, that they have sunk to their present position.

The Chandala agitated for over thirty years for a change of the nomenclature which was turned down by the authorities repeated on the advice of the pundits. Since 1901, they made more organized and determined attempts on this behalf. It is interesting to note that between 1911-1931; most castes of Bengal including Baidyas and Kayasthas demanded a change of caste nomenclature. In 1911, the total weight of the voluminous representation to the govt. was over 1 ½ mounds. The relation between the Chandals and the high caste Hindu was so strained and ill feeling ran so high that in 1911 they represented to the British Govt. for grant of treatment of the caste at par with the Muslims and demanded separate privileges.

Due to this concept, the Namasudra people fought against the so-called caste Hindus of India long back during the 19th century for their social recognition and against social humiliation. In the early part of this year (1873) the Chandals made a general strike in the District of Faridpur (presently in Bangladesh) resolving not to serve anybody of the upper class, in whatever capacity, unless a better position among the Hindu caste than what they at present occupy was given to them (Hunter, 1876). It was against the social humiliation and persecution that the Namasudras observed a 'general strike'. In addition, this is the country's first general strike. The report of C A. Kelly, ICS, District Magistrate, Faridpur in this behalf discloses thus. 'In the early part of this year (1873) the Chandalas made a general strike in the District of Faridpur (presently in Bangladesh) resolving not to serve anybody of the upper class, in whatever capacity, unless a better position among the Hindu caste than what they at present occupy was given to them'.

Since the 1880s the efforts of the Chandalas to change their nomenclature to Namasudra are noticed. F.B. Peacock, Commissioner, Presidency Division writes in a letter [No.87 dated Alipur, the 18 July, 1881] that 'The improvement in the conditions of the Chandalas who are in the chief agriculturists in Narail subdivision [of Jessore District] has led them.......to aspire to a superior status in the Hindu caste system. They called themselves Namasudra and profess to be Baishnab. W.C. Macpherson, ICS, Assistant Commissioner, communicated the order of the Deputy Commissioner, Sylhet thus: 'that Namasudra must always be written not as Chang or Chandala for all persons of the said caste that Deputy Commissioner has ordered that any person who does not write Namasudra shall be removed from employ. On a memorandum submitted to the Chief Commissioner, Assam by some prominent social activists of Cachar district for change of caste name from Chandala to Namasudra, his secretary [letter No.2195 dated 19th August, 1885] says '........ the chief Commissioner sees no objection to person to call themselves Namasudra being designated as such in official documents. Nevertheless, their prayer for a change of caste nomenclature from Chandala to Namasudra was not allowed due solely to the opposition of the orthodox Hindus. In 1911 the Bengal govt. affected the change to Namasudra by a notification.

In this regard, the revered Namasudra socio-religious leader of Faridpur G C Thakur may be mentioned. Gourchand Thakur fought against the so-called caste Hindu for changing their name as Namasudra instead of Chandala in 1893.

This Chandalas got recognition as Namasudra from the British Govt. in the year of 1885. It is worthwhile to mention that in Assam the Namasudra people migrated from Bangladesh long back and settled in Assam and living permanently and some of them have adopted Assamese culture as well. The British Govt. used the term 'depressed caste' to identify so-called untouchable castes experiencing socioeconomic, cultural discriminations at the hands of the upper caste people. In 1931, Ambedkar submitted a memorandum at the second roundtable conference to change the term 'depressed classes' into 'Scheduled Caste'. This was due to the fact that the erstwhile untouchables objected to the 'depressed class' term. The term 'Scheduled Caste' was adopted in 1935 to provide some social, economic and political safeguard to the section of the people who were being deprived socially, politically and economically at the hands of the upper caste people.

Although the constitutional commitment is there to provide a safeguard to the scheduled caste people still that safeguard is hardly implemented and executed. The Government of India is making a lot of efforts to implement it but, at the same time, the politics is initiating counter-productive caste system by way of creating other backward class, which leads to half of the population of the country to become backward and schedule. Thus, attempt should be made to overcome these barriers by way of creating consciousness among the people in general through education and the scheduled caste or the other backward communities to have education and become conscious to utilize the opportunities equally among themselves without becoming creamy layer, for which only government effort is not sufficient rather, public involvement is indispensable.

References

Annual Administration Report, Presidency Division, 1880-81 quoted by S. Biswas, p. 275.

Bandyopadhyay, S., 2005, 'Caste, class, and politics in colonial Bengal: A case study of the Namasudra Movement of 1872-1937', In KL. Sharma (Ed): *Caste and Class in India,* pp. 408, Rawat Publications, New Delhi.

Bhagabat Gita, Chapter-4, Sloka-13.

Bhuimali, A., 2007, *Development of Schedule Caste*, pp. 160, Serials Publications New Delhi.

Biswas, A.K., 2000, *The Namasudras of Bengal*, pp. 6 – 7, Blue Moon Books.; New Delhi:

Biswas, U.N., 2004, '*The Strike*', pp. 48, NCMB Memorial Trust; Kolkata.

Das, B., 1986, *A Glimpse of the Schedule Castes in Assam*, Omson Publications; New Delhi.

Ghurye, G.S., 1996, *Caste, and Race in India*, Popular Prakashan, Bombay.

Hasnain, Nadeem., 1991, *Tribal India Today*, pp. 8, Harnam Publication; New Delhi.

Hunter, W.W. 1876, *Statistical Account of Bengal*, Vol. VI, Trubenor, and Co; London.

International Encyclopaedia of Social Sciences, p. 333.

Paswan, S. and J. Pramanshi 2004, *Encyclopaedia of Dalit in India Social Justice*, pp. 7, Kalpaz Publications; Delhi.

Sarkar, Gourprio. 1995, *Jatitatta Sangraha*, pp. 36, Hiranmay Sarkar, North 24 Pargana, West Bengal.

Sarkar, Sattya Ranjan, *Namasudra Jatitatttwa* (Bengali), p. 3-4.

Sarkar, Shukhamay, 1382 (Bengali Year), *Namasudrai Parsav Bipra*, pp. 81, Khulna Press; Bangladesh.

Singh, K.S., 1995, *The Scheduled Caste*, pp. 978, Oxford University Press; New Delhi.

CHAPTER - 10

DE-SANSKRITIZATION MOVEMENT IN MANIPUR

M. C. ARUNKUMAR

One of the most controversial social movements in Manipur is the Meitei de-Sanskritization movement which was started during the colonial days. The movement is otherwise known as *Sanamahism*, Meitei Revitalization or Meitei Revivalism. To a section of revivalist groups, the movement is known as *Pakhangba Laining*. The movement is described by many social scientists, historians as a religious movement (Singh, 1982). However, a few historians (Singh, 2012) take such movement as a social movement having certain political goals taking such movements are a response to the emerging colonial and feudal nexus in the State. The movement dates back to the first quarter of the 20th century which witnessed the British colonial division of hill and plain administration, the limited power of King of Manipur in socio-cultural activities in the valley areas. The King could not take any political decision but be given more or less unlimited power relating to religious practices at that time. Though the Hindu elements in Manipuri culture (especially of the Meitei) can be traced back to early days of Manipuri history, the ancient Meitei religion could have its own independent system. The cultural elements, including those of different religions, could be synthesized in the body cultural.

The Meitei system had a dramatic change since the days of the late 17th century. The Meitei society started to become a Hindu society gradually. The Meitei experience of the Hindu wave of the time is categorized by M Kirti Singh (Singh, 1980) into two periods: the first period covers the reign of Charairongba and Garibniwaz. During this period, *Nimbarkism* and some earlier forms of *Vaishnavism* flourished; and then came *Ramanadi* from Sylhet. In the second stage, *Gaudiya Vaishnavism* appears as the State religion under King Jayasimha. From this time dates the existence of Caitanya school as a powerful sect through some records assign it to a much earlier. In the later period, the people's recollection of the historical event in which forceful conversion to Hinduism is one of the vital forces in the de-Sanskritization movement. The conversion of the masses took place on Sunday, Meitei lunar month of *Ingen* (June-July) of 1738 AD. They were enjoined not to take or touch meat and wine after a ceremony, called *Nongkrang Iruppa*. He decreed to bury nine *Umang Lais* on *Kalen* of 1726; broke the images of seven *Umang Lais* in Inga of 1726; burnt as many as 120 ancient texts (Singh, 1980). The society became a Hindu society, though there were a few resistances from some quarters of the population. The days were described by one of the noted Manipuri historians in Manipur, Prof Gangmumei Kamei: Propagation of a new religion (*Ramanadi*) was started with full vigour after 1720 under the active guidance of Shanta Das. The king gave charity to all the Brahmins and astrologers. In *Phairel* 1725, the tombs of the former kings, queens and princes and princesses were opened and the skeletons of the dead bodies were exhumed and cremated again. The ashes were immersed in the Chindwin River. There was an objection to the opening of the tombs as it was a sacrilege for the Meitei according to their religious customs. These objections were overruled by the King (Kabui, 1991).

After the Meitei embraced Hinduism, there was a process of synthesis of the traditional religion and Hinduism. It was not that the traditional religion was replaced by the Hinduism.

Saroj Nalini Paratt observed that the two systems of religion were distinct and separate entities. Coexistence there certainly was, but the degree of religious synthesis evidenced in the records makes it impossible to view the religion of the period simply as two distinct faiths existing side by side. There was a much greater emphasis on integration both of the Meitei lai into the Hindu system and of the Hindu gods into Meitei culture (Paratt, 1960).

With the conversion of the Meitei to Hindu society, the society was stratified on the basis of castes. Caste hierarchy was newly introduced with Brahmin migrants and marginalized social groupings. By this period, Brahmins had been assimilated; they were no longer regarded as *Mayangs* (Paratt, 1960). *Mayangs* are those people coming from westward, especially from mainland India. The Varna system could not be fully introduced because of historical reasons, but the society had Brahmin (*Bamon*), Kshetriya and exterior caste, *Loi*. The Brahmins who reached Manipur at different times, however, were subjected to Manipurinization. They were assigned certain family names and went through a process of Manipuri acculturation. The Meitei conversion of Hinduism and its social change has its own uniqueness. The migrant Brahmins were transformed to Meitei *Bamons*. The earlier gods and goddesses, deities and other ancestor spirits were incorporated along with Hindu gods and goddesses. In short, the Meitei religious system has two domains: Hindu domain and Meitei traditional domain. The two have their independent practices even after the society became a Hindu society.

The Meitei society witnessed another introduction of socio-religious categories of *gotra*. The Meitei has seven clans (*yek*); besides it, the Hinduized Meitei society followed *gotra*. The *yeks* were assigned corresponding *gotras* as follow:

	Yek	***Gotra***
1.	*Ningthouja*	*Shandilya*
2.	*Angom*	*Kaushika*

(Contd...)

3.	*Chenglei*	*Bhardwaj*
4.	*Luwang*	*Kashyap*
5.	*Khuman*	*Madhugalya*
6.	*Moirang*	*Aitereya*
7.	*Khaba-Nganba*	*Gautam*

The two systems of Meitei religious life have their own spheres and these systems follow their respective cosmological and ritual practices independent of each other. However, there is a long process of assimilating each other's elements. Because of it, the Hinduism in Manipur could evolve into Manipuri Vaishnavism in the second half of the 18th century within the larger Vaishnavite sect of Chaitanya School. The synthesis of the two religious systems was described by S K Chatterji: 'Manipur Hinduism gradually became a synthesis of the old Meithei with its gods and goddesses and myths, its own legends and traditions, its social customs and usages, and its priest and ceremonials, and of Brahminical Hinduism with its special worship of Radha and Krishna' (Chatterji, 1950).

The religious practices of the Meitei had a turn after the British occupation of Manipur in 1891. In September 1891, the question of the future of the Manipur State was decided by His Excellency, the Governor General in Council. The Government of India declared that the Manipur State was forfeit to the Crown, but decided in their clemency to re-grant it to a scion of a junior branch. Their choice fell upon Churachand Singh. He was not entitled to be King of Manipur in the normal line of descent. He was minor at the time of coronation. On 18 September 1891, a *sanad* was issued (Singh, 1997). After the attainment of the age of majority, he became a full-fledged king within the principle of indirect colonialism.

In his reign, as the entire administration was controlled by the Political Agents and Durbar, his power was limited to a smaller sphere. He could levy tax and duty without the approval of Durbar only in certain areas, especially from matters related to customs and religion. One of such tax was

Chandan Senkhai which is levied from the Hindu Manipuri (Meitei) for using *Chandan*. The tax gave a heavy burden to all the Meitei families. There was a strong sense of discontent among them. Another burden was the strict imposition of religious rules on *mangba* and *sengba* (pollution and purity). Those who did anything against any religious rule were declared as polluted (*mangba*); the polluted persons were excommunicated from the community. Even they were not allowed to be cremated unless purified. During the period of excommunication, a dead body had to remain for days without cremation. Even relatives would not come to an invitation from an excommunicated person. For the ritual of purification (*sengdokpa*), they had to pay a certain amount of money.

Among the Brahmins (*Bamons*), there arose ill-feelings. When the Raja and his family came into the possession of the idol of Govindaji, which was the god of the reigning Manipur Prince, the family priests or Brahmins were preferred to the royal temple, and the former Brahmins who officiated in the post in continuity were dismissed. The latter was known as *Aribas,* and the new Brahmins as *Anoubas,* the distinguishing words meaning 'old' and 'new' respectively (Singh, 1997). The trouble between the two groups of Brahmins was finally closed during the 1890s.

The game of *mangba* and *sengba* was played by *Brahma Sabha*, the apex body of religious matters, under the patronage of the king. The *Brahma Sabha* used to exercise power and influence of the Brahmins with the patronage of the Maharaja. The decision of the *Sabha* was the last verdict on many social and religious issues. The authority of the *Sabha* was utilized more on the formal side of religion than for the spiritual content of the Hindu faith. The *Brahma Sabha* soon became an instrument for exploitation and misuse of the royal power in the name of religion during the colonial period.

It became, thus, unpopular among the social reformers. It was only after 1934 when the *Nikhil Hindu Manipuri*

Mahasabha came into existence that the imposition of *mangba* and *sengba* had faced political opposition.

Many Manipuri, in whose name the *Brahma Sabha* declared *Mangba,* could not pay their fines opted to remain as *mangba*. There was a strong sense of discontent among the people; gradually they started to revive their pre-Hindu religion though in low profile. What was believed was that lest they are not Hindus, they would be outside the sphere of *Brahman Sabha*. Or they opted to be *Lois,* the exterior caste outside the *Varna*. These individuals gradually started a movement among the *mangba* persons in defiance with the rules and norms of *Brahman Sabha.* As the king of Manipur was strong enough in customary and religious matters, they could not mobilize enough resources for a social and political movement.

The *anti-Brahman Sabha* feeling became stronger day by day, but the people of Manipur could not resist in an organized way as the nexus of the King and British colonial administration was so strong that the people could not speak out or protest anything due to strong repressive measures. However, a few individuals tried to start a movement for de-Sanskritization of Manipur religion – to remove Hindu elements from the 'synthesized' Manipuri religion. They started to perform Meitei rituals and worship the Lord Pakhangba, not Hindu gods and goddess. In doing so, they did not require any service of Manipuri Brahmins (*Bamons*). Some of these pioneers in de-Sanskritization of Meitei religion were closely associated with the King and his council. They studied and kept the *puyas* (ancient texts). It was their duty to interpret and advise the king to act in a given situation. These individuals did not like the activities of *Brahma Sabha*; though they wanted to launch a movement against the *Brahma Sabha*, they did not like to negate the King's authority. Thus, a group of such individuals worked hard to study the literary history of ancient texts (*puya*) in order to understand the archaeology of knowledge of the Meiteis.

Another interesting development in the religious life of the Meitei was the social movement for using Manipuri in *Kritans* and *Sanskritan*. A group of Hindu scholars translated many Bengali and Sanskrit texts into Manipur and used different hymns and performed ritual performances in Manipuri. This was against the Bengali chauvinism and was compounded with a new political consciousness. The new spirit of Manipuri nationalism emerged in the 1920s and 1930s. The language movement in the religious domain was, in a sense, a revolt within the Manipuri Vaishnavite system. This reform movement fueled further to the camp of de-Sanskritization.

The movement that had been started by a few individuals was in a colonial situation where the king did not have much political power. The King and Brahma Sabha were so repressive that the voice of resistance could not be strong and loud. On the other hand, the Meiteis in Assam started a new search of Meitei identity in Bengali dominated Cachar and adjourning areas. The tyranny of the Manipuri king and British Political Agent was absent in Assam. However, the Manipuri Hindus in Assam found themselves alienated with Bengali chauvinism. In the situation, though less exposed to rich ancient texts and a long history of *puya*-based knowledge, a movement was launched by Naoria Phulo who was once in Assam police service. As he was a British subject in Assam, he could organize individuals who wanted to distinguish themselves from Hindus (especially Bengalis) in Assam. Again, as he was outside the sphere of *Brahma Sabha* of Manipur, he had not experienced what Manipuris in Manipur experienced *mangba-sengba*. He started a movement called *Apokpa Marup* in 1930. There is a difference in the meaning of *Apokpa* (ancestor) between the Naoria Phulo's group in Assam and its Manipuri connotation in Manipur. *Apokpa* (ancestors) in Naoria's meaning includes all the ancestors and progenitors of the Meitei including Sanamahi, Pakhangba who were sons of Sidaba Mapu (Almighty God); whereas, *Apokpa* is considered as the progenitor of a particular lineage. Every lineage worships and offers ritual items which differ from one lineage to another on a fixed date in Meitei lunar calendar. *Apokpa* is the most important deity of a lineage; in the hierarchy of supernatural beings, above the *Apokpa* are other gods and goddess. There was a group of people under the banner of *Pakhangba Marup* which aimed to revive the cultural legacy of pre-Hindu Meitei culture since 1933. Leaders of the group had been kept under the bar in 1938 for about a month.

In the State of Manipur, formal associations called *Meetei Marup* and *Meitei Marup* were established around 1945 (Hodamba, 2012). This is the time when the nexus of King and Colonial agents was a threat from an external force. The advancing Japanese army became a visible threat to the British and Raja rule. The iron hands of the colonial rule became weaker with various social and political movements in those days. Many social and political groups of different colors, from liberal to communist, started different movements in the State. The two revivalist groups became more active in the post-colonial period. Though the revivalist groups which were offshoots of these two groups aimed to achieve de-securitization of Meitei religion, their attitudes towards Manipuri Hinduism are quite different. Hence the history of the revivalist movement in the postcolonial or post-merger period in Manipur history has different hue and shades. The hue and shades based on their outlooks on (a) anti-Hinduism (from simple denial to aggressive attack on Hindu elements in Meitei society), (b) anti-Indian domination (from a group taking anti-Hindu is anti-India to another group anti-Indian domination has nothing to do with Hinduism, (c) national liberation (searching ethnic identity of the Meitei to quest for the restoration of lost national pride).

The nomenclature of the movement is varied from one region to another or one group to another. In the early days, it was seen a big debate over the naming of the movement, ranging from *Apokpa* (following followers of Naoria Phulo) to

Pakhangba Laining to *Sanamahism*. Today, a large number of people accept *Sanamahism* to name the movement, though opposition is there. Another group of people likes to name the movement as a simple movement of Meitei religion.

In Manipur, the movement gradually gains its momentum in the post-colonial period when the king and his men of *Brahma Sabha* ceased to use repressive measure in the name of *mangba-sengba*. The most visible moves in the de-Sanskritization movement in the Meitei society are the change of content of the rites de passages. Though the forms of ritual performances are more or similar to those of Manipuri Vaishnavism, the meanings and contents of the performances are different. The Hindu gods and goddesses are not invoked and the Brahmins are no longer the ritual specialists in these de-Sanskritzed performances.

During the process of conversion to Manipuri Vaishnavism, many traditional gods and goddesses, deities were identified as Hindu gods and goddesses. For examples, *Nongpok Ningthou* was identified as Shiva, *Panthoibi* as *Durga*, *Hingyangthang Lairembi* as *Devi*. As the de-Sanskritization movement advances, the revivalists started to de-recognize the identification and to worship the traditional gods and goddesses with non-Hindu rituals. With it, in many sacred places, there come up two parallel systems of worshipping as revivalist and Meitei Hindus perform their own rites and rituals.

A constant movement is organizing Meitei festivals – de-Sanskritized or new festivals – to give a new meaning of Meitei festivals from those of the Manipuri Vaishnavism. These festivals attain momentum with wider participation and elaborate religious and festive elements. One such festival is that of *Cheiraoba* festival on the first day of Sajibu, the first lunar calendar of Meitei calendar. The Meitei Hindus celebrate *Cheiraoba* following Bengali calendar. Though the forms of celebration of the two *Cheiraobas* are more or less similar, the meanings are quite different. Many more rituals are performed elaborately.

Two festivals, *Imoinu Iratpa* and *Panthoibi Iratpa*, become more accepted by the general populace. Imoinu, the goddess of Wealth, is worshipped on the 12th day of Wakching (a 10th month in lunar calendar; it falls in December and January) at the fireplace of a family. The worshipping of Imoinu became public festival since the early days of the 1970s and special attractions had been added gradually day by day. The government of Manipur declared the day of Imoinu Iratpa as a restricted holiday in 1993 and became a full holiday since 2000. It can be noted that the involvement of masses across the boundary line of their religious beliefs is obvious. It is because of the achievement of the revivalist movement as well as the duality of Meitei religious practices.

Likewise, the Panthoibi Iratpa is gaining its momentum in attracting general masses. The Panthoibi Iratpa is performed during the Durga Puja of the Meitei Hindus. Goddess Panthoibi was worshipped in a festive environment. The starting point of the Panthoibi Iratpa as a festival is obscure but is believed to have been started in Thangmeiband area by some revivalists (Singh, 2012). The festival, initially, aimed to replace the Durga Puja; but the two festivals are organized in various areas side by side.

Now the de-Sanskritization movement gains various socio-political connotations, ranging from new revivalist wave to asset Meitei identity to nationalist movement of the Manipuris. The theological issues to metaphysical exercises are compounded with a new wave of Meitei-ness and Manipuri nationhood. The de-Sanskritization movement that started in a colonial period when the King with limited power and the indirect rule of the British repressed the masses with various state apparatuses enters a new phase with many more political connotations. But, the dual practices of Hinduism and traditional religion that show the unity of Meitei religion cannot be broken down; hence de-Sanskritization is still a challenge for various revivalist groups.

References

Chatterji, SK 1950 ' Kirata-Jana-Kriti'. *Journal of the Royal Asiatic Society of Bengal* 16: 288.

Hodamba, ND 2012. 'Waakoklon Hilel Thilel Salaai Amaailon Pukok da Mityeng'. Ama: http://hodamba.blogspot.in/2012/09/waakoklon-hilel-thilel-salaai amaailon.html, retrieved on 30 July 2017 at 11 pm.

Kabui, Gangmumei. 1991. *History of Manipur* Part I. Akansha Publishing House; New Delhi.

Parrat, Saroj Nalini. 1960. *The Religion of Manipur*. Firma KLM; Calcutta.

Singh, Karam Manimohan. 1997. *History of Christian Missions in Manipur and the Other Neighbouring States*. Mittal Publications; New Delhi.

Singh, M Jitendra. 1982. 'Meitei revivalist movement in the 20th Century'. In JB. Bhattacharjee (Ed): *Proceedings of the Northeast India History Association,* pp. 200-205. Northeast India History Association; Shillong.

Singh, M Kirti. 1980. *Religious Development in Manipur*. Manipur State Kala Akademi; Imphal.

Singh, N Joykumar. 2012. *Religious Revitalization Movements in Manipur*. Akansha Publishing House; New Delhi.

CHAPTER - 11

A RELIGIOUS MOVEMENT OF TINGKAO RAGWANG CHAPRIAK AS RESPONSE TO CHRISTIAN CONVERSION

AKHUAN GANGMEI RONGMEI

Introduction

The onslaught of Christianity brought a tremendous change especially in their religious life of the tribals of Northeast India. In Manipur, one of the Northeastern States, it came after 1891 when the British conquered the State. The British, under the Arthington Aborigines Mission, sent one young missionary named William Pettigrew in 1894 to proselytize among the Meiteis, a major community of Manipur. He learned Bengali and Manipuri (Meiteilon). A Porom Singh was believed to be the first Christian convert among the Meiteis of Manipur. However, on the stern objection by the orthodox Hindu community, Arthington mission has shifted from the valley of Manipur and Pettigrew was advised to work among the Tangkhuls of Manipur. He worked there for 25 years. He did pioneering works there. He started a school, doing evangelical works, learning the Tangkhul Language and studied the customs and religious beliefs. Students from different communities such as Tangkhul, Meitiei, Kuki, Kom, and Anal joined the school of Pettigrew at Ukhrul. These students became Christian evangelists. They were sent to different places of Manipur to proselytize the people. The Kuki evangelists, Teba Karong and Longkhovel Kom and others did evangelical works in south-east and northwest of part of Manipur hills. Pettigrew's mission was successful among the peoples who were not strongly influenced by the Hinduism and other religions.

After Pettigrew, the British sent Rev. U.M. Fox, another missionary to Manipur in 1911. With the permission of Maharaja Churachand Singh, he entered Ukhrul. Rev. Fox somehow penetrated into the valley of Manipur, which is the forbidden land to the missionary works, and converted five State Government employees including Maipak Kabui into Christians in 1915. Manipur State Durbar was strongly against this conversion and rejected any sort of construction and location of churches in the valley. Amidst this resistance, the Manipur Christian Association was formed in November 1916. Maipak Kabui was the first Christian convert among the Kabuis of Manipur. His life story makes an inspiring and worth reading. Church historian Namthiurei narrates a brief biography of Maipak. 'Maipak was born at Khaukin village in Tamenglong. His mother died young and so he was brought up by his father. An epidemic occurred in the village and the villagers shifted to Aling. Later his family came down to Imphal and settled at Keishamthong in search of livelihood. Maipak as a young man started working as a carpenter. He worked in the Residency of the political agent, who was impressed by his skilled craftsmanship and sincerity. Through the recommendation of the political agent, Maipak was employed in the palace of Maharaja Churachand Singh. The Maharaja noticed the young carpenter and recruited him to the State Police and he became a palace guard. Maipak was quite talented and joined the Maharaja's band. The Maharaja was impressed with his music and he was ultimately appointed the bandmaster of the Maharaja's police. And he lived at Keishamthong which was the colony of the employees of Manipur State Police, band party and palace guards. Maipak and his wife Pantigongliu did not have any child and very much saddened by the issue less marriage. He talked the matter with a bandmaster of Sadiya, who suggested that he might have children if he accepted Christianity. Maipak started meeting Christian converts from Ukhrul. He conversed with two evangelists, Teba Karong and Longkhovel and studied the Bible in Manipuri. In 1914, he and his wife embraced Christianity. The family was blessed with a son whom he named David Kaphunlung, seed of life.

As noted above Maipak and his five friends were baptized at Imphal creating a furor between the Manipur State Durbar and the Mission. Maipak and his friends built a small thatched hut at Keishamthong village for worship. This was called the church. Rev. Pettigrew used to visit the church and meet the new converts, the villagers of Keishamthong were not happy with the conversion of Maipak and his Christian activities. On January 19, 1916, the second group of converts was baptized by Rev. Pettigrew himself. They included the wife of Maipak, Pantigongliu, Thenjeilu Lunsili Abung and Angou. Later on, the Maharaja was outraged at the conversion of his favorite bandmaster into Christianity. His displeasure compelled Maipak to give up his lucrative and influential job. He started going around Imphal taking the message of Christ. In 1920, he and his friends were shifted to Thangmeiband.

In 1918, Maipak went to Oinamlong on the old Cachar road to preach in a police outpost. He met Jinlakpou of Kaikao, who accepted Christianity. While Maipak was the first Kabui convert, Jinlakpou was the first Zeliangrong convert of Tamenglong region. During the Kuki rebellion, which spread to Tamenglong Hills, Maipak continued to preach despite the opposition from the followers of the traditional religion. He visited anal villages also. In 1922, Rev. William Pettigrew whose mission headquarters was shifted from Ukhrul to Kangpokpi sent Maipak to Kaikao to lead the first Christian group there. He came to Tamenglong Headquarters to work as a carpenter and settled there to continue the evangelical works. Namthiurei observes, his life was a prayer. He never cared for his personal gain. He lived an exemplary life. He had sown the first seed of the Gospel among the Zeliangrong people in the area. He was a real carpenter repairing the broken souls tirelessly up to the end of his life'. He passed away on June 9, 1944, at Tamenglong (Kamei, 2004).

The case of Maipak Kabui indicates that the juggernaut of Christianity came with the tools of modernization, education and technical training, publication of literature in the language of the converts, giving medical help and employment both in the mission and colonial government. These were the persuasive strategies to which the hard life tribal people and the people who were living in subsistence economy became an easy prey. This technique was successfully adopted by the missionaries. They also accepted western culture and civilization which are based on scientific technology as a superior civilization. Moreover, Christ's teachings were spread through churches, schools, bible or written words, modern medicine, and technology, relief and welfare activities.

On the other hand, the tribal religion which is fundamentally polytheism could not withstand Christian condemnation of their religion as an animistic cult which was full of orthodox and superstitious practices. Their indigenous concept of the Supreme Being, *Pathian* among the Mizos and Kukies, *Tingkao Ragwang* among the Kabuis, which is similar with the essentials of God of Christianity, cannot be properly asserted due to the lack of organization and proper authority as such. The testimonies of the native converts also served as a vanguard for conversion to new religion. On the top of that, the ignorance of the true essence of their religion and its philosophy was easily overwhelmed by Christian doctrines of a millenarian life in heaven, living in God's kingdom.

However, the traditional tribal religions were not silent at all. They strongly resisted the conversion. They even started to assert that every conversion is a loss of old faith. Among the Kabuis, some resistances took the negative courses. Severe persecutions were reported in different parts of the State. The first kind of persecution was reported in Kaikao village in 1923-24 where the new Christian converts were asked to leave the village. In 1938, another incident of persecution occurred at Tamenglong in Manipur. Similar persecution was faced by the Christians of Sempang in 1951 when they moved back to Kaikao ancestral village. When they were constructing a house of worship, they were attacked by non-Christians and eventually three Christian's leaders were killed and eleven injured.

Another incident of alleged beating up of new Christian converts was reported at Chingmeirong Rongmei colony on 13th July 2006. Three families who were converted were asked to leave the village and ex-communicated. The problem is not yet solved even today. There are much more Kabui Christians who are persecuted in many forms and degrees. And some resistances take a course of strengthening the traditional religious system to move ahead towards an organized religion. Among the Kabuis, the religious movements of TRC Heraka in the colonial period and Champa and TRC in the post-colonial period are such a conscious movement which negates Christianity as well as molding the traditional religion into organized religion.

Heraka

Heraka is a synthesis of Christian monotheism and Hindu idolatry and temple culture. It literally means 'pure' in Zeme. It is a reformed traditional religion introduced by Haipou Jadonang. The true essence of this religion was revealed in the dreams of Haipou Jadonang and his disciple Rani Gaidinliu during their pilgrimage to Bhuban cave which is located at Cachar, Assam. It is believed in one Supreme God traditionally known as *Tingwang*. This Supreme God created the universe, sun, moon, earth and other cosmic objects. *Heraka* is monotheism. It does not believe in the worship of spirits or smaller deities. Sacrifices to small gods were abolished. The goal of *Heraka* is to bring good and prosperous life to men individually and collectively through the grace of God. *Tingwang* is worshipped by singing the hymns and songs on every full moon day. The Hera cult has simplified the birth, marriage and death ceremonies. *Gennas* and taboos were abolished. But the propitiation of *Tingwang* through the construction of *Tarangkai* and performance of *Banru* are still followed. Marriage ceremonies have been modified and simplified. *Heraka* had village level association and used an earring as a symbol.

Haipou Jadonang revitalized and simplified the form of worship of God. He preached the mode of worshipping God. He not only abolished different types of taboos and *gennas* in the society, but he also started the temple cult and idol worship. The temple is traditionally known as Kao Kai consisting of a shrine, pulpits, and aisles of bamboo. Such temple was first constructed at Kekru, then at Kambiron, Nungkao and Binnakandi in Assam. He also composed many devotional hymns and songs which are famous among the Kabuis. He taught that sacrifice of animals was not the only way to Tingwang. After the arrest and execution of Haipou Jadonang, his disciple Rani Gaidinliu continued his reform movement. In 1960, there was a clash between her followers and the Naga underground on the question of the profession of religion. She was a great saint patron of *Heraka* cult. Even after imprisonment, followers continued to worship her.

Genesis of *TRC*

The geography of *Heraka* cult is very much limited. It is concentrated in some Zeme and Liangmei areas of North Cachar Hills and Nagaland, and Tousem Sub-Division of Tamenglong of Manipur. Lack of strong religious authority, organization and religious books or code of rites of passage, etc. may be the reason for decreasing its popularity among the people.

But the legacy of pilgrimage and frequent religious congregations at Bhuban Hills gave an opportunity for public discussion on this issue. Ultimately they organized a public meeting under the leadership of Maringa Maringmei of Ragailong Imphal, to discuss their religion on 8 March 1993. The meeting expressed a great need for the formation of a religious authority to preserve, study, and systematize their traditional religion and also to propagate their belief, customs, and tradition. It was also expressed a great concern over the conversion of religion.

A steering committee was formed to organize the conference on traditional religion. And the traditional customs and religion protection committee was abolished. After one year of the intensive mass campaign, the conference was held at Imphal on 14-16, April 1994. This historic conference was attended by 1500 delegates from Assam, Manipur, and Nagaland and unanimously resolved the following issues

(i) Establishment of the apex religious authority known as the *Zeliangrong Ra-Chapriak Phom* (Zeliangrong Religious Council) with a constitution.

(ii) Declaration of the name of religion as *Tingkao Ragwang Chapriak* through the ritual of *Lougai Karikmei*(chanting the name of God holding a sacred hoe).

(iii) Every religion requires a God, an organization, and a name.

(iv) The religious council has to publish the texts of hymns, songs and the rite of passage known as the *Ringlon* and *Theilon*.

(v) The construction of a place of worship and there should be community or mass prayer in every village on every full Moon Day

As a result, the council now manages most of the religious affairs of the people which were earlier managed by a council of elders known as Pei. It has compiled the rites connected with birth, marriage, and death, and published the same in form of a sacred book entitled *Ringlon-Theilon* (rites of passage). It has become a scripture of the faith. The council not only had published hymns and prayer for different occasions, it also issued and distributed cassettes to the villages. They sent volunteers to teach these songs. They abolished the taboos on unnatural deaths of the community and every dead person should be treated with honor and provided with usual rites of passage.

Moreover, the Council constructed a house of worship traditionally known as *Kalumkai* at Chingmeirong Kabui village and established the ecclesiastical council, women and youth fellowship each serving different functions in the council. The youth wing organizes training camps and imparts knowledge to young men and women of the society. The council organizes prayer meeting on every full moon day and Sunday at the *Kalumkai*. It has become a place of religious congregation and pilgrimage. This religion is now a member of the international United Religious Initiatives based in San Francisco, through the Manipur Co-Operation Circle.

Philosophy of *TRC*

Historically speaking, there was no conscious effort to give a name to traditional religions. So was the case with many of the world religions. Hinduism, Judaism, Buddhism, Christianity, etc. evolved through times. The need for a specific name of the religion was felt by every section of the society. Though there was the practice of believing gods and goddess, it was not organized to identify as a distinct religion. A concrete identity of faith in its relation to other world religion is needed to be established. *Heraka cult* and *Champa* are such earlier efforts of the community. And ultimately the religion *Tingkao Ragwang Chapriak* is a fruit of consistent efforts of the community.

It was named after the supreme God, *Tingkao Ragwang*, which is worship by the Kabuis. *Tingkao Ragwang* literally means heavenly supreme God. Prof. Gangmumei argues that TRC is a primordial religion. He refuted the used of notions like animism to describe indigenous tribal religion by the Westerners. He further argued that the terms like primeval and primordial religion are more appropriate and accurate to define indigenous tribal religion.

Primordial religion means a religion with a primordial existence since the beginning of time, ancient and eternal. It is almost equivalent to Sanskrit word *Sanatan Dharma* meaning an ancient and eternal religion. TRC is thus a primordial religion of the Kabuis, a religion practiced and followed by them since the creation. This religion has polytheistic and henotheistic features because it worships god and goddess and at the same time it believes in the supreme God as the highest God out of many gods.

The fundamental doctrines of *TRC* are as follows,

(i) Belief in supreme god, *Tingkao Ragwang* who is the creator of the universe, gods, and men, who are benevolent and protector of men. He is Omniscient, Omnipresent and Omnipotent.

(ii) Belief in the existence of many gods and deities who are assigned by the heavenly god to look after the different aspects of the world, nature, and humans.

(iii) Belief in the concept of heaven, the abode of God, *Tingkao Ragwangkai* or *Tingkao Kaidai* and the life after death represented by the land of the dead (*Taroilam*) where man's soul goes after death.

(iv) Belief in the worship of the deities presiding over the villages and places (*Shong* and *Bambu*) to act as the guardians deities of men in these villages.

(v) Belief in the concept of the ancestor worship (*Kairao Kalummei*) and in the concept of the rebirth of the human soul.

(vi) Worship of Gods (*Ra Kalummei*) and propitiation of the lower deities (*Ra Khangmei*)

(vii) Belief in the concept of sin which is locally known as '*Non*' as deviation or violation of the religious, moral and social customs and norms and retribution by God for the same.

(viii) Belief in the performance of the rites of passage relating to the birth, membership of social institutions, marriage and death (*Ringlon-Theilon*)

(ix) Belief in the redemption and salvation of the soul in heaven for good doers and retribution by the divine for bad doers.

(x) Belief in the performance of festivals, ceremonies and rituals and other forms of religious and cultural expression of the worship of the divine.

These tenets or doctrines clearly establish the *TRC* as a well-formulated distinct religion with a well defined theological foundation.

The Concept of Supreme God or Heavenly God

The *TRC* is basically based on the fundamental belief in the supreme God, *Tingkao Ragwang*. It literally means the heavenly god or god of the sky or lord of the universe. He is worshipped as the supreme god, the creator of the universe, nature, gods, men, and animals. *Tingkao Ragwang* hymns and rites are endowed with all the divine elements ascribed to God.

(a) *Tingkao Ragwang* is eternal, no beginning and no end

(b) He is the creator of the universe

(c) He is benevolent and good

(d) He is the source of life, giver of the soul and the ultimate goal of the human soul

(e) He is the architect of man's destiny

(f) He is holy and source of holiness

(g) He is the source of knowledge and wisdom

(h) He is described and known by different names expressing the infinite versatile power of the divine

(1) He is called *Tingkao Ragwang*, the heavenly God.

(2) He is *Shamting Phianmei*, one who plaited his hair (as men chant his name the plaited hair fall apart)

(3) *Tingwang*, god of the heaven or sky.

(4) He is *Somprai Gwang*, king of the gods worshipped by men (*Somprai* means the creator of the uncreated and destroyer of the created)

(5) He is *Pashumeipu Padammeipu*, the creator of men.

(6) *Tamshumeipu* and *Tamjanmeipu*, the ordainer of the need of humankind.

(7) *Tingpuk Kandi Kasemmeipu*, maker of the sky and earth.

(8) *Kachak Dandi Pannumeipu*, wearer of gold and silver.

(9) *Bu Nei Dammeipu,* creator of the moon and sun.

(10) *Bushinmeipu Budammeipu*, giver, and protector of soul.

(11) *Himdaimeipu*, wielder of power, the almighty.

He is thus, eternal. He has no beginning and no end. He has no beginning, no end. He is not created. He creates out of nothing by his will. He has no father, no mother. He just exists. He is benevolent, dispenser of welfare and prosperity to men. He is the creator of soul and the ultimate god of the soul. He is really omniscient, omnipresent and omnipotent.

The Symbol of *TRC*

The Council adopted a symbol traditionally known as *Boudan*. The symbol consists of a circle, Criss-Cross lines and image of sun and moon. The circle in the symbol represents the universe or cosmos created by the God. The Criss-Cross lines denote the zodiac in the sky. The moon and the sun symbolize his creation in the sky. This symbol is widely used in any occasion of worship of *Tingkao Ragwang*.

The Concept of Soul

Soul in *TRC* is the essence or animating element of

individual life. Presence or absence of a soul is the indicator of life or death of a person. It is *Tingkao Ragwang* who gives soul to the man. He is traditionally described as *Businmeipu Budammeipu*, the ordainer, and protector of the soul. The soul is the source of all energy for maintaining the body. Soul emanates from *Tingkao Ragwang* and the goal of a soul is *Tingkao Ragwang* himself. In *Tingkao Ragwang Chapriak*, it is believed that the soul in the body sometimes can be moved outside the body and can call back the soul to return to the body. It is traditionally known as *Bukaomei*.

Since the soul comes out of God, it is presumed to be holy. However, as it resides in the body, it is subjected to the good or bad effect on the action, thought and mind of the man. That is why soul enjoys suffers the effect of the good or bad action of the man he or she lives.

After death, the soul will go to the land of the dead, *Taroilam*. From there, the good, uplifted and holy soul will go to heaven. Sinners will stay in the land of the dead for some time and will be reborn in the human world. In *TRC*, there is no concept of hell but sinners will born and reborn and die until it is born into degenerated life forms. Thus the ultimate goal of the soul is heaven, *Tingkao Kaidai*.

Heaven

The *TRC* believes in the existence of heaven which traditionally known as *Tinkao Kaidai*. They also believed that heaven is in the sky. It is the wish and dream of every believer to go to heaven when she or he died. It is believed that everything is there. There is no suffering, pain, hunger, jealousy, and anger but full happiness and peace. It is a place for those who committed no sins in the human life and those who strictly follow the doctrines of the *TRC*.

It is also believed that the performers of religious ceremonies like *Ragaidai, Bamjou Kimei, Ragai Jeisan, Muleng Kimei Banru and Tarangkai Sumei* will go to heaven after death. The devotees of *TRC* must follow the following advice to enable them to enter heaven after death.

(i) Strictly follow the teachings of *TRC*
(ii) Listen to teaching and stories of *TRC*
(iii) Offering and sacrifices to *Tingkao Ragwang*
(iv) Offering charity under the name *Tingkao Ragwang*
(v) Love and help the poor
(vi) Don't hurt a man physically and mentally
(vii) Don't tell a lie and steal
(viii) Be polite to everybody
(ix) Don't show the vanity
(x) Don't commit incest and adultery
(xi) Be just while making a judgment
(xii) No jealousy
(xiii) Be truthful and good to others

Life after Death

The *Tingkao Ragwang Chapriak* believes in the existence of the land of dead, *Taroilam.* No one exactly knows where it is. But it is believed to be the bowl of the earth. It is also believed that there is a god named *Taroigwang*, the king of the dead who looks after the affairs of *Taroilam.*

He makes a judgment on the souls coming into his kingdom based on their past actions, the commitment of sins, and worship of *Tingkao Ragwang* while they are living in the physical world. Those souls who are free from any sin, the performance of duties towards *Tingkao Ragwang*, the performance of prescribed ceremonies and sacrifices in the name *Tingkao Ragwang* will be sent to heaven.

Moreover, it is also believed that those who are sinners or evil doers are punished by him. And they sent back to the land of living to be reborn according to their deeds. A relation between the world of the living and the land of the dead is maintained through the medium of shaman priests and dream diviners.

Sin

It is the deviation from or violation of the accepted spiritual, social and moral norms of the society. It is locally known as *Non*. A man commits the sin is punished by God and society. The divine punishment is in the form of death, the transformation of his or her soul into lower forms of life like animal, insect, and plants. However, in *TRC*, there is a ritual for the redemption of one's sin or wrongdoing.

Mode of Worship

The worship of *Tingkao Ragwang* ranges from the chanting of his name to the performance ceremonies and sacrifices.

(*i*) *Neimei* (*genna*): It is a form of collective prayer to *Tingkao Ragwang* by abstaining from any work in the village. It is observed for plentiful harvests. It is also observed to ward off any danger from natural calamities due to earthquake, hailstorm, fire, attack of pests, insects, and rodents in the paddy fields.

(ii) The performance of religious ceremonies like *Ragaidai, Ragaidai Jeisan, Bamjou Kimei, Muleng Kimei, Banru and Tarangkai Sumei.* These ceremonies are based on the ideal of charity to all and pleasing the people and perform to obtain divine blessings and to attain salvation.

Festivals

Among the Kabuis, there are nine festivals. They are *Gan Ngai, Ri Ngai, Nanu Ngai, Napkao Ngai, Ginki Ngai, Gudui Ngai, Tun Ngai, Pukpha Ngai*, and *Dongjao Ngai*. All these festivals are related to the worship of *Tingkao Ragwang*, the Supreme God. Traditionally, the believers of *TRC* worship the Supreme God, to give well-being, prosperity, happiness, fertility, the longevity of life, etc.

Conclusion

Tingkao Ragwang Chapriak is an evolved religion of the Kabuis. It is a response to proselytization in the post-colonial period. Though it negates Christianity, it synthesizes some elements of Christianity and Hinduism in molding their traditional belief system as an organized religion. In short, Christianity can sometimes, be seen as a boon in disguise. They have now temple to worship, scriptures, code books, and religious authority which controls everything in the society. Yet, this religion still calls for more collective effort, zeal, scientific temperament, a wide canvas to absorb more devotees from different corners of the world.

References

Kamei, Gangmumei, et al. 2013. *The Philosophy of Zeliangrong Religion: Tingkao Ragwang Chapriak.* Tingkao Ragwang Chapriak Phom; Imphal.

Kamei, Gangmumei. 2004. *A History of Zeliangrong Nagas From Makel to Rani Gaidinliu.* Spectrum Publications; Delhi

Kamei, Gangmumei. 2005. *Tingkao Ragwang Chapriak: The Zeliangrong Primordial Religion.* The Zeliangrong Religious Council; Imphal.

Kamei, Gangmumei.1997. *Jadonang A Mystic Naga Rebel.* Lanshailu Kamei Publications; Imphal.

Kamson, Chaoba. 2009. *Tingkao Ragwang Chapriak Ra Pari.* Jashillu Publication; Imphal.

Kamson, Chaoba. 2011. *The Philosophical Concept of Tingkao Ragwang Chapriak.* Tingkao Ragwang Chapriak Phom; Imphal.

Kamson, Chaoba. 2012. *Thousumei Kasoi Kadam.*Tingkao Ragwang Chapriak Phom; Imphal.

Kamson, Chaoba. 2014. *Maku Banru Khatni Tarang Laangpatmei.* Ganglaona Family Publication; Imphal.

Longmei, Longphun, 2012. *Zeliangrong Kaku Lon.* The Tribal Research Institute; Imphal.

Pamei, Ramkhum. 1996. The *Zeliangrong Nagas: A Study of the Tribal Christianity.* Uppal Publishing House; Delhi.

Phaomei, Kambuilung. 2011. *Phaomei Gaiganglung Panti Pari*. Tingkao Ragwang Kariak; Imphal.

Remei, Marulung. 1995. *Kasoi Khatni Kadam*. Remei Publication; Imphal.

CHAPTER - 12

WHY MIGRATION A THREAT TO THE PEOPLE OF MANIPUR?

SOUGAIJAM PRIYOKUMAR MEITEI

Introduction

Migration is regarded as the change of one's residence due to certain forces. A simple theory is that it takes place in search of better opportunities or searching for better conditions. Theoretically, migration results in advantages to both places of origin and destination. Everett Lee (1969) opines that migrations are always selective, never purely rational and all migrants do not migrate as a result of their own decision. Migration is an impact of social forces in response to meet the growing demands of an individual or a group. The advantages so far incorporated with migration are macro-level researchers and are universally accepted. In European countries and the US, there are several types of research, many policies about how to promote, build the capacity of the migrants to increase economy. Poverty has been considered as one of the important factors of migration, and the problem is to some extent reduced through migration and in return, their services to industries play a distinct role in industrial growth. This means that migration is a factor of positive economic change and plays a pivotal role in the spatial distribution of population over time. Human Development

Report (2009) also argues that migration and development go hand in hand. It further stated, 'Mobility can facilitate access to ideas, knowledge, and resources that can complement and in some cases enhance progress.' Bogue (1959) considers migration as 'an instrument of cultural diffusion and social integration, which yields more meaningful redistribution of the population'. However, there is always a room for conflict embedded between the local people and the newly arriving people because of various reasons. The reasons are region specific and need to be assessed.

Migration can be again positive or negative on both the source as well as the destination areas. Migration may be of various types according to nature and patterns, temporary or permanent, internal or international, legal or illegal, forced or voluntary and so forth. Apart from these types, the United Nation has also identified a form of migration which is categorized into irregular migration. The migration that occurs outside of the rules and procedures guiding the orderly international movement of people is the irregular migration[1]. Irregular migration poses multiple challenges to countries of origin, transit, and destination, as well as to migrants' themselves[2] (International Migration Policy, 2013).

Irregular migration in Northeast India is an ongoing problem to the general public of this region. Migration in Northeast India is filled with a number of conflicts, agitations and ethnic tensions. The 'Bangladesh factor' is an important issue in Northeast India due to illegal migration from Bangladesh (Mehrotra, 2009). Many of such cases of migration in Northeast India may be treated as irregular migration. These factors and impacts of migration are not a new phenomenon in the Northeastern part of India creating various social tensions, time and again. Irregular migrants have basically forced migrants, refugees or displaced population due to ethnic conflicts, resource occupancy, and natural disaster primarily crossing the international line of borders.

The present chapter focuses on the social movement in Manipur relating to migration. Manipur is one of the states of Northeast India. It was a princely state which has two thousand years long history. Undoubtedly, migration took place in the state since that time. However, we need to have the history of migration right after the formation of Manipur by the indigenous hill and valley people. The Meitei and Pangals reside in the valleys while several tribes are settled in the hills of Manipur. The arrival of the Bengali and their assimilation in Meitei society during Maharaj Khagemba in the 17th century is a remarkable historical migration. Those migrants particularly Bengali Brahmins and Bengali Muslims were absorbed into the Manipuri society. In the earlier times, migration being a small stream was not significant to create any social problem. Many Nepalis were also arriving during the king's time. The king allowed them to settle by providing plots of land. Even the village name was given in their Nepali language such as *Char Hajar, Kala Pahar*. There is evidence where the Nepalis also joining some position in Manipuri king's court. The migrants, thus, either by assimilating or integrating into the host society, the Manipuri nation has been formed.

A Small Multi-Cultural State

Manipur is a very small state of Northeastern India. Many of its areas have got poor demographic data due to unhealthy law and order; poor transport system, isolated and are hilly regions at large. Manipur shares a very small population in India. Sex ratio and the literacy rate are nearly equal or better with the national average. Manipur has been resided by a number of ethnic groups inclusive of migrants and original peoples. Among the major migrant communities, the Nepalis, the Bengalis, the Punjabis, the Telis may be significantly noted. The state has a very pleasant climate and rich in forest resources. From the very past, the state has a better economy, demography, political lives than that of Bangladesh, Burma, and Nepal. Urmila (2002) rightly pointed out that India's neighbours are poorer than India. Therefore, once the migrants arrived in Manipur, they wish to continue for permanent settlement. Meanwhile, the state has no proper policy to maintain the undocumented arrivals.

The arrival of the British in Manipur is again another landmark. They accompanied Indian traders, clerks, army men etc. The existing history of Manipur clearly indicates that the then king and people of Manipur warmly welcomed those migrants with proper regards and respect. Initially, the king of Manipur had a friendly relationship with those Britishers. However, the arrival of the British, after knowing the colonial eyes, the people of Manipur acquired a resistance feeling towards the migrants who were accompanied and arrived later.

After the departure of the British, those followers of Indian origin continued to settle since they had started making space and places into the soil of Manipur. They started claiming themselves as the sons of the soil. Their size of the population was not large at all during the earlier times. But the most problem in Manipur is these early arrivals have been mixed up with the later arrivals and the indigenous people of Manipur refer them collectively as *Mayang*, because of completely different cultural traditions – food, dressing, rites, and rituals etc. The new migrants and the earlier ones are sure to have a different sense of inclusion, nationalism relating the sense to embrace Manipur as their motherland. The early arrivals were not a problem, were welcomed by the then people. However, the late arrival when the state has got a structural imbalance becomes a social tension. The Marwaris, so widely expanded in the business sector of Manipur is needless to mention since the same is true for the whole national picture. The Bengalis are usually the descendants of those bureaucrat officers accompanied by the Britishers. The Telis were traders dealing grocery items employed by the Britishers when there was the intention to introduce a capitalist market in the state.

The migrants arrived to give assistance to the Britishers or as servicemen of the British administration. This orientation has brought a big confrontation to the host egalitarian society. It is because, through these migrants, information flew to their place of and facilitated the passage of new kins, friends, and relatives. The census indicated a huge volume migration in Manipur during post-independence period. The migrants who arrived in Manipur before merge were foreigners since they were covered by the Foreigners Act of the constitution of Manipur (1947). Once the Act was revoked (1949), people's attitude toward Indian subjects could not be instantly removed and thus continued. These migrants have been distinctively known as the *Mayang* people. The *Mayang* is a foreigner mix up with the people of Manipur. The concept of being a foreigner to the people of other Indian states could not be removed readily by a mere merger agreement (merge to the Indian Union) signed by King Bodhchandra at Shillong. It is believed that the agreement was signed under pressure sidelining the will of the people and stakeholders of Manipur.

Trends in Social Movements

Over time many new ethnic groups mix up with and they fell into the description of '*Mayang*' meaning mix population. Presently, the migrants and their children have acquired a huge size such that the number has created insecure and a threat to the indigenous people of Manipur. This is not a simple phenomenon of xenophobia. At the international level, no universally accepted definition of xenophobia exists, though it can be described as attitudes, prejudices, and behaviour that reject, exclude and often vilify persons, based on the perception that they are outsiders or foreigners to the community, society or national identity. There is a close link between racism and xenophobia, two terms that can be hard to differentiate from each other[3] (https://www.iom.int/key-migration-terms). The concept of xenophobia is hardly applicable in case Manipur. The Mayang is a part of the majority population in the context of mainland India. So they may or may not feel the sense of minority in the state. This is sure to create them a dual identity in their ways of life and status. Moreover, their population in Manipur is suddenly increased to a much larger extent. It is the reality that the number of *Mayang* people is more than the Schedule tribe population of Manipur in 2001 census (United Committee Manipur, 2005). The main demand of the people of Manipur is to develop a lively mechanism or strategy to distinguish the *Mayang* people based on their base year of arrival in Manipur. There are several rooms of confusion in identifying and distinguishing the early and the later arrivals among the migrants due to lack of records and proper documentation. For example, the foreigner arrived before one day of the merger agreement became no longer a foreigner immediately on the next day. This is the existing gap between the logical and technical reasoning. That is why; people treated them as a foreigner and the same feeling still exist.

Migration and associated problems are not merely a temporary political game rather they are the sequential shocks people had encountered over time. Migration in Manipur unlike universal optimistic view has never brought economic growth. Moreover, the migrants in Manipur are not classified properly, not properly verified. Internal migration is not illegal, is promoted as a basic right by our Constitution. However, the redistributing nature should be checked to make it more rational and meaningful. In migration theory, there is stream and counter stream and make the population distribution balance in its natural setting. But, it is not always true because migration is determined by multi-dimensional factors – poverty, war, famine, development-induced displacement, personal, psychological, conflicts etc. Conflicts and communal disharmony are very frequent in Bangladesh and Myanmar which could be one of the reasons we the Northeastern state receive a large size of the irregular and forced immigrants.

Going back to a recent history, several agitations and movements rise up in Manipur reacting to migration since British time. One famous historical event *Nupi Lan* meaning women war (the second *Nupi Lan*), took place on 12 December 1939. It was an artificial famine created jointly by the Britishers and traders from some other Indian states. Since then, the whole state business sector has been controlled by these migrants and their generations. There are hundreds of reasons why people have felt the sense of xenophobia, insecure to its socio-economic and cultural ways of life as because of the heavy flow of population. A definite policy on migration taking the initiatives by the state government will be quite beneficial for the safety and security of the people.

There are many pieces of evidence of illegal immigration into Manipur. But no constructive measure so far has been introduced in the state. The Joint Committee on Inner Line Permit System, Kangleipak claimed that 71.5percent of the total voters in Jiribam Sub Division are migrants from different parts of India and other countries. Therefore, it is the right time to understand the contemporary threats felt by people of Manipur as because of population influx and to highlight the growing social pressures upon it. The United Committee Manipur (2005) published a book 'Influx of Migrants into Manipur – A Threat to Indigenous Ethnic People' had given a view to identifying the original population composition hailing Manipuri National Subgroups of the state of Manipur.

Recently, several organizations claim to enact the Inner Line Permit (ILP) System in the state from the viewpoint of the protection of indigenous people and its culture. Manipur is having high decadal population growth since 1901 according to Census, India; it is always higher than the national rate. Census of 1961, following the abolition of ILP system, revealed that the decadal growth rate of Manipur was tremendously high at 35 percent against the national growth rate of 22 percent only. Manimohon in his one of the writings (2008) has opined that migrants from outside the state should be categorized on the basis of their nature of activities and duration of their stay and they may be issued some sort of official token or card for identification. His idea is about to introduce a means to check and control the unnecessary and unwanted illegal migration in future which may be detrimental to the social, economic and political stability of the state.

The Bubble Point

At different intervals of time in Manipur, there are social upheavals sprouted in the different community-based organization for the protection of the original people of Manipur. These migrants and the children of these migrants were not properly enumerated at the time of the merge, and hence these people were mixed up with the later arrivals that are considered as internal migrants. Therefore, there is always a technical problem in sorting and classification of the type of migrants in Manipur. This is how we are entrapped in between the technical and logical meaning of *Mayang* and indigenous people or sons of the soil. It is a continuing debate the chronological generation of the migrants to be included in the category as the sons of the soil. Manipur had experienced a series of mass movements on foreigner issue. Several civil society organizations, student bodies were taking the issue seriously and started movements. The All Manipur Students Union (AMSU) had taken a deserving role in delineating the misery of illegal immigration in Manipur. The All Manipur Students Union (AMSU) had taken a pioneering role in reporting that there is an influx of foreigners from Bangladesh, Nepal etc based on certain data. Urmila (2002) wrote a clear stand and roles of AMSU over foreigners' issue. It was found that in Manipur, based on 1971 census, the decadal population growth was much higher than the national average. That decadal growth of India was 19 per thousand while it was 37.53 for Manipur in this year. It may be noted here that birth rate of Manipur is always lower than that of the national average. The AMSU keeping these statistics in their mind, filled with emotion and sentiment, started movements to convince the people rationally.

The foreigner's issue was brought up during the 1980s and still, it is going on. The initiatives taken up by student activists are really helpful in making political consciousness and mass integrity. The recent movement spearheaded by Joint Committee on Inner Line Permit System (JCILPS) in 2015 on foreigners issue is also a sparkle of the uncompleted students' movement in the past. It demands that the Inner Line Permit System or a similar type of permit system should be implemented to all the migrants arrive in Manipur in 1951 as base year of identification. The migrants' position in the business sector is quite notable. When there is an economic blockade in Manipur, *Mayang merchants,* they sell goods at their desired price; they do not face the problem of stock out. They have a strong connection with political leaders through their investments at elections and at other intervals. The JCILPS joining hands with various students' wings, Local Clubs, Meira Paibis (Local level women organization a transformed association of *Nishaband* means banning of intoxicating substance) started the movement vigorously for two months long in the year 2015 (July-August). People organized mass rallies; sit-in protest, general strikes, hunger strikes, human chain, road blockade, burning of effigies. State security forces were busy enough to control the various types of agitations. They used tear shells, mock bomb, water cannon, blank fire, and *lathi* charge. During the agitation, a student of class XII standard named Robinhood was killed by rubber bullet of security forces. It was the flickering tragedy in the history of Manipur that a stronger agitation with full of sentiments came into the picture of the social movement. Many government offices, vehicles were destroyed. The government could not stay silent any longer with the bursting out the scenario and ultimately decided to fix the solution. The state government along with JCILPS, an agreement was made to pass the bill after two months long protest.

It was unfortunate that instead of putting up the issues on a higher debatable platform, the matter is transformed into several agitations, strikes, and curfews, mass rallies affecting to the general day to day lives of the people. No one is allowed to give critical comments in opposition to the movement since mob justice is prevalent in some areas of Manipur. This is a sign of emotional movement working on sentiments without knowing the essence of professionalism. That is why such movements which are carried forward by much emotion with less reason usually end up without a positive outcome. The famous Sepoy Mutiny could not get success because the reason for the revolt was not for freedom, it was not planned and not well managed and not having a true leader. The same case is the agitations in Manipur against the foreigners' issue. Therefore, the agitations hardly transform into the success of the demands made. There are several issues in Northeastern India associated with the emotional sentiments behind the shadow of ethnicity or ethnic identity and struggle for land occupancy. For every movement in Manipur, it indirectly or directly affects the life of another ethnic community. No movement so far underpinning with a sense of nationality or integral identity is emerged. Contrarily, the movements by an ethnic community opposed by another ethnic group, the movements by some CBOs, opposed by another organization has been continuously appearing in the state. The movements rose up by the JCILP after signing an agreement with the state government, the bill for Inner Line Permit system with 1951 as base year was passed in the Legislative Assembly. It was immediately reacted to Kuki tribes and revolted against it accusing the government that their Hill Area Committee was not concerned before; this bill will disturb their land area. Base on several charges, the Kukis of Churachandpur district started many civil disobedience agitations, and at the time of confrontation with the state security forces, nine protesters had lost their lives. As a result, the bill for Inner Line Permit system passed by State Assembly has been rejected by the President of India.

Conclusion

A big problem of population infiltration is persisting in Manipur for a long time directly or indirectly through porous international borders. Due to its ill-border and improper demarcation, the Manipur-Myanmar border, is currently having a serious dispute over it. People now feel insecure about their ethnic culture, economy, and political lifeways as because of huge population influx. Therefore, people are demanding to enact a law in the state to regulate the same. Even the majority people, the Meitei group perceive they are on the verge of extinction unless there is a constitutional safeguard for this people. This assumption has been considered less significant by the politicians and administrators and the issue remains unsolved for several decades. The threat level needs to measure properly to make the possible co-existence.

Migration is a problem when the host society feels population pressure with respect to economy, politics, and culture. It is the time to uncover the veils by regulating the porous floodgates of several flights to prevent unwanted infiltration and to safeguard the host community from being jeopardized. Practical inputs need to be imposed by the state authority rather than pleading Utopian type of appealing. Xenophobia is another problem in the state which can be negotiated through the integrative process. Migration should be positively translated as a corridor to development, as well as a way forward to the multi-cultural nation. The different civil organization claimed that the indigenous people will be paralyzed socio-culturally if the free influx is not checked in time. The demand is all for the need of both the indigenous people and the migrants. If it is misinterpreted to the migrants as if the demand is against the migrants, then it will be like oil and water in the same vessel. At the same time, a proper safeguarding rule for the migrants should also be taken up to curtail any kind of communal tense in Manipur.

Finally, one question is deep rooted to the people of Manipur toward the mix-up population. A Nepali migrant, named Kishore Thapa, elected as Member of Legislative Assembly (MLA) of Kangpokpi Assembly Constituency (AC) in 1974 was really a striking example. This was the first shock to the political scenario to feel a sense of insecure to the mass people. Following this, the second shock is a subject of Bangladesh origin Ashab Uddin elected as MLA of Jiribam AC. We have foreigner issue for the subjects of Nepal, Bangladesh, and Burma. Till now, we have witnessed the shocks relating to Nepali and Bangladeshi immigrants. Now the big question is 'shall we wait for the third shock of the similar type from Burma origin or so? Shall we do something to prevent or to protect the original people of Manipur?' Illegal migration is a quite visible form in India and will remain a security challenge if there is no immediate delineation of the migrants.

References

Bogue, Donald J. 1969. *Principles of Demography*. pp 752-823, John Wiley and Sons; New York.

Lee, Everett S. 1969. 'A theory of migration' In JA. Jackson (Ed.) *Migration*. pp 282-297. University Press of Cambridge, Cambridge.

Meetei, Manimohon, 2008, 'Migration in Manipur', *National Geographer*, Vol. XLIII, 1 and 2: 123-142.

Mehrotra, Mansi, 2009, *Illegal Immigration in India's Northeast: Perennial Problem*. Centre for Land Warfare Studies, (CLAWS)

United Nations Development Programme 2009, *Human Development Report 2009: Overcoming Barriers: Human Mobility and Development,* Palgrave Macmillan, Basingstoke and New York.

Urmila, Ningthoukhongjam. 2007, *Student Movements in Manipur*, Akansha Publishing House, New Delhi.

1. http://www.rcmvs.org/documentos/IOM_EMM/v3/V3S12_CM.pdf Retrieved on 5/5/2017.
2. http://www.un.org/en/development/desa/population/publications/pdf/policy/InternationalMigrationPolicies2013/Reportpercent20 PDFs/k_Ch_5.pdf Retrieved on 5/5/2017.

3. https://www.iom.int/key-migration-terms Retrieved on 5/5/2017.
4. International Organization for Migration, Retrieved from www.iom.int/about-iom.

INDEX

B

S